Children's
FIRST
Encyclopedia

Children's

FIRST

Encyclopedia

p

Author and Editor
Neil Morris

The publishers would like to thank the following people for their help:
Suzanne Airey, Jenni Cozens, Pat Crisp

This is a Parragon Publishing Book
This edition published in 2001

Parragon Publishing
Queen Street House, 4 Queen Street,
Bath BA1 1HE, UK

Produced by Miles Kelly Publishing Ltd
Unit 11, Bardfield Centre, Great Bardfield, Essex CM7 4SL

Hardback ISBN 0-75255-650-9
Paperback ISBN 0-75256-574-5

Printed in China

Contents

Introduction

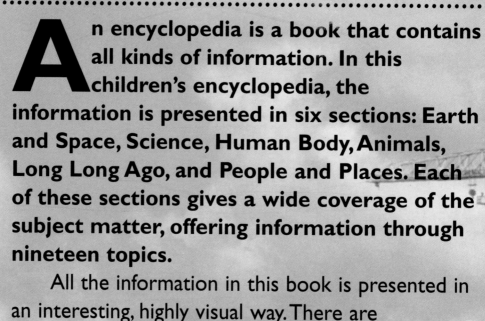

An encyclopedia is a book that contains all kinds of information. In this children's encyclopedia, the information is presented in six sections: Earth and Space, Science, Human Body, Animals, Long Long Ago, and People and Places. Each of these sections gives a wide coverage of the subject matter, offering information through nineteen topics.

All the information in this book is presented in an interesting, highly visual way. There are hundreds of photographs, illustrations, and even cartoons, all with explanatory text. Extra captions offer fascinating facts. Of course, no encyclopedia of this size can possibly cover every topic, but the

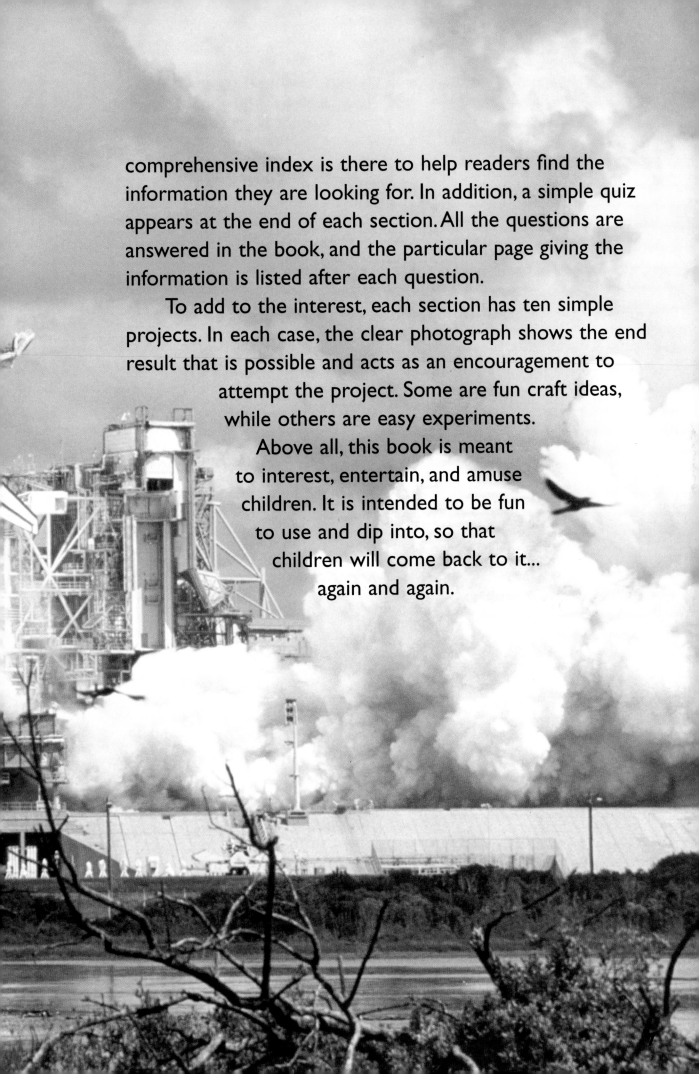

comprehensive index is there to help readers find the information they are looking for. In addition, a simple quiz appears at the end of each section. All the questions are answered in the book, and the particular page giving the information is listed after each question.

To add to the interest, each section has ten simple projects. In each case, the clear photograph shows the end result that is possible and acts as an encouragement to attempt the project. Some are fun craft ideas, while others are easy experiments.

Above all, this book is meant to interest, entertain, and amuse children. It is intended to be fun to use and dip into, so that children will come back to it... again and again.

How to use this book

In this book, every page is filled with information on the sort of topics that you will enjoy reading about.

Information is given in photographs and illustrations, as well as in words. All the pictures are explained by captions, to tell you what you are looking at and to give even more detailed facts.

Illustrations are clear and simple, and sometimes they are cut away so that you can see inside things. The triangle at the beginning of the caption text points to the illustration concerned.

Captions beginning with a symbol give extra pieces of information that you will find interesting.

The cartoons throughout the book are not always meant to be taken too seriously! They are supposed to be fun, but the text that goes with them gives real information.

Project boxes describe craft activities related to the topic. These are things to make or simple experiments to do. The photograph helps to show you what to do, and is there to inspire you to have a try! But remember, some of the activities can be quite messy, so put old newspaper down first. Always use round-ended scissors, and ask an adult for help if you are unsure of something or need sharp tools or materials.

Mountains

There are high mountains all over the world. They took millions of years to form, as the plates that make up the Earth's crust squeezed and buckled.

Mountain ranges that lie near the edge of plates are still being pushed higher. They have steep, rocky peaks. Older ranges that lie further from the plate edges have been worn away over the years by rain, wind, and ice.

It is cold on high mountains, and the peaks have no pl

New Words
△ **crag** A steep piece of rough rock.
△ **range** A group or series of mountains.
△ **strata** Layers of rock.

△ **The Earth's plates are** made up of layers of rock, called strata. As the plates move, the strata are bent into folds. In the mountains, you can often see how the layers have been folded into wavy lines.

△ **Block mountains** are created when the Earth's crust develops cracks, called faults, and the chunk of land between them is pushed up.

△ **Mountains** are often joined together in a series, or range. The longest and highest ranges, such as the Andes and the Himalayas, form huge mountain systems. Few animals or people live on the highest mountains.

△ **Dome mountains** form when the top layers of the Earth's crust are pushed up by molten rock underneath. This makes a big bulge.

△ **Fold mountains** are formed when one plate bumps and pushes against another. Rock is squeezed up into folds. The Andes were made this way.

What is an ibex?
The ibex is a wild mountain goat that lives in the high mountains in some parts of the world. Ibexes are sure-footed and happy to climb along rocky crags. Male ibexes have long horns, which they sometimes use to fight each other.

MOUNTAINS OF JUNK
Crumple newspaper into big balls and tape them onto a cardboard base. Make papier-mâché pulp by soaking newspaper pieces in a bucket of wallpaper paste. Cover the balls with the pulp to make mountains and valleys. When your landscape is dry, paint some snow-capped peaks with white paint. Sprinkle the base with sand. You could add a mountain lake.

△ **The ten highest** mountains on land are all in the Himalayas, to the north of India. The highest peak of all, Mount Everest, lies on the border between Nepal and Tibet. It is 29,028 feet (8,848 m) high and is known to people of Tibet as Chomolongma, or "goddess mother of the world."

▷ **The longest** mountain range on land is the Andes, which stretches for over 4,500 miles (7,000 km) down the west coast of South America. The Transantarctic Mountains stretch right across the frozen continent of Antarctica.

The main text on each double-page spread gives a short introduction to that particular topic. Every time you turn the page, you will find a new topic.

Beautiful photographs have been specially chosen to bring each subject to life. The caption triangle points to the right photograph.

A New Words box appears on every double-page spread. This list explains some difficult words and technical terms.

EARTH AND SPACE

Our home, **Earth**, is just one of the nine planets that travel around our star, the Sun. And the Sun is really just an ordinary star, like many millions of others in the Universe. Scientists already know an enormous amount about the Universe and space, and yet there is still much more to learn in the future.

On Earth, there are interesting things to see and learn about, from rocky mountains to deep oceans, and from thick forests to sandy deserts. Some of the things we humans do every day are threatening to spoil our planet, but we can all help to make the world a better place.

Our Planet

We live on the planet Earth. On our planet there are high mountains and hot deserts, huge oceans and freezing cold regions. A blanket of air is wrapped around the Earth. This air allows us to breathe and live. Beyond the air, our planet is surrounded by space. A long way away in space, there are other planets and stars. Most planets have satellites, or moons, which circle around them.

△ **From space, Earth** looks like a mainly blue and white planet. It looks blue because water covers most of its surface. The white swirling patterns are clouds, and the brown and green areas are land.

Earth has a diameter of about 7,900 miles (12,700 km), almost four times bigger than the Moon. The Moon is about 240,000 miles (385,000 km) away from Earth.

The Moon circles the Earth once a month. On its journey, different amounts of its sunlit side can be seen from Earth. This makes the Moon seem to change shape during the month.

△ **The Moon spins** as it circles the Earth, so the same side always faces us. People had never seen the other side of the Moon until a spacecraft traveled around it.

🌍**asteroid** A miniature planet.

🌍**crater** A round dent in a planet's surface.

🌍**diameter** The width of a circle or ball.

🌍**satellite** A planet that travels around another planet or a star. Earth is a satellite of the Sun.

△ **The Moon** was probably formed when a huge asteroid crashed into the Earth billions of years ago. The crash threw rock fragments into space, and these came together to form the Moon.

▷ **The Moon's surface** is full of craters. These were formed by chunks of space rock crashing into it. There is no air or water on the Moon, so it is odd that we call the Moon's vast, dry plains "seas."

The Solar System

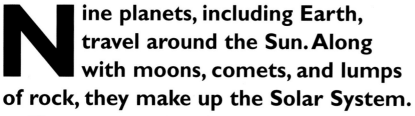

Nine planets, including Earth, travel around the Sun. Along with moons, comets, and lumps of rock, they make up the Solar System.

This system is Earth's local neighborhood in space. Everything in it is connected to the Sun by a force that we cannot see. This force is called gravity.

The largest planet, Jupiter, is big enough to hold over 1,300 Earths. The smallest planet, Pluto, is smaller even than our Moon.

▽ **Among the planets** there are four giants— Jupiter, Saturn, Uranus, and Neptune. Each has a small rocky core, surrounded by a thick layer of ice or liquid, with gas on the outside. Along with Pluto, these giants are called the outer planets.

Mercury

Venus

Earth

Mars

PLASTICINE PLANETS

Mold Plasticine around beads, marbles and ping-pong balls to make planets. Earth can be blue and white, Mars red, and Jupiter orange. Mold a big yellow Sun around a tennis ball. Use black cardboard for a space background and arrange the nine planets in the right order. You could put a label next to each one.

Jupiter

Pluto

Neptune

Saturn

Uranus

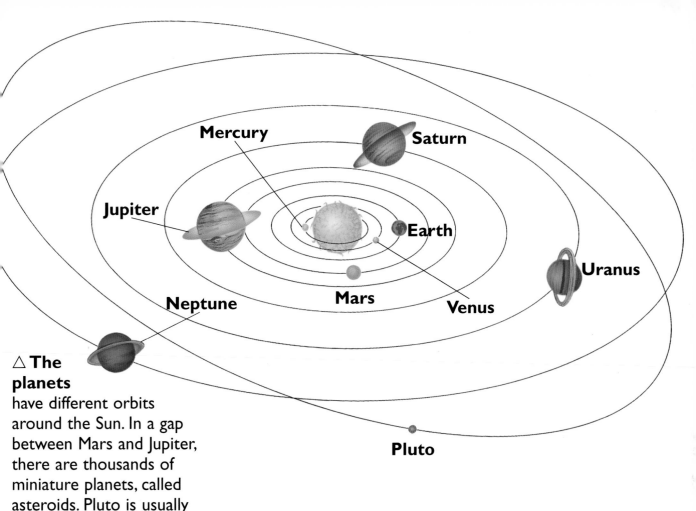

Mercury

Saturn

Jupiter

Earth

Uranus

Neptune

Mars

Venus

Pluto

△ **The planets** have different orbits around the Sun. In a gap between Mars and Jupiter, there are thousands of miniature planets, called asteroids. Pluto is usually the farthest planet from the Sun, but sometimes its path crosses Neptune's.

Mercury is a small, rocky planet. It is closest to the Sun and travels around it six times in one of our Earth years.

NEW WORDS

comet A snowball of ice and dust that travels around the Sun.

gravity A force that pulls everything toward it.

orbit To travel around something.

solar To do with the Sun.

PLANETS NAMED AFTER GODS

Mercury, messenger of the gods

Venus, goddess of love

Mars, god of war

Jupiter, king of the gods

Saturn, father of Jupiter

Uranus, god of the heavens

Neptune, god of the sea

Pluto, god of the underworld

13

Our Star

Aquarius,
the Water-carrier,
Jan 20-Feb 18

Pisces,
the Fish,
Feb 19-Mar 20

Aries,
the Ram,
Mar 21-Apr 19

Taurus
the Bull
Apr 20-Ma

Our Solar System has one star, which we call the Sun. Stars burn, and the sunlight that gives us life is the light of our burning star.

The Sun is a vast, fiery ball of gases. The hottest part of the Sun is its core, where energy is produced. The Sun burns steadily and its energy provides the Earth with heat and light. We could not live without the Sun's light, which takes just over eight minutes to travel through space and reach us.

You must never look directly at the Sun. Its light is so strong that this would harm your eyes.

Twinkle, twinkle, little star
Seen from Earth, stars seem to twinkle. This is because starlight passes through bands of hot and cold air around the Earth, and this makes the light flicker. In space, stars shine steadily.

photosphere

sunspot

▷ **Heat from the core** surges up to the Sun's surface, called the photosphere. Sunspots are dark, cooler patches. Prominences are jets of gas that erupt from the surface.

14

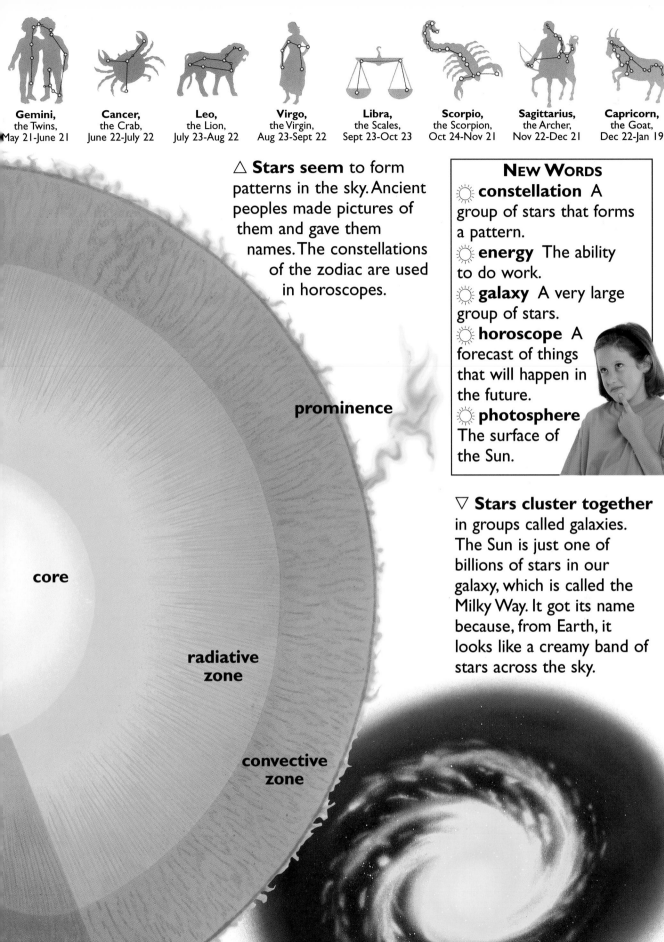

Gemini, the Twins, May 21-June 21

Cancer, the Crab, June 22-July 22

Leo, the Lion, July 23-Aug 22

Virgo, the Virgin, Aug 23-Sept 22

Libra, the Scales, Sept 23-Oct 23

Scorpio, the Scorpion, Oct 24-Nov 21

Sagittarius, the Archer, Nov 22-Dec 21

Capricorn, the Goat, Dec 22-Jan 19

△ **Stars seem** to form patterns in the sky. Ancient peoples made pictures of them and gave them names. The constellations of the zodiac are used in horoscopes.

prominence

core

radiative zone

convective zone

▽ **Stars cluster together** in groups called galaxies. The Sun is just one of billions of stars in our galaxy, which is called the Milky Way. It got its name because, from Earth, it looks like a creamy band of stars across the sky.

15

▷ **Scientists believe that** millions of years after the Big Bang, gases clustered into clouds. These clouds clumped together to form galaxies.

The planets formed later from clouds of gas, dust, and rocks. As the Universe expands, the galaxies are moving farther apart.

galaxies form

△ **There are countless** billions of stars in the Universe. Sometimes a very old star explodes. We call this a supernova. New stars are being created all the time in different sizes.

▽ **The Sun** is an ordinary yellow star. It is much bigger than a red dwarf star, which is half as hot. A blue giant is at least four times hotter than the Sun. A red supergiant is five hundred times the Sun's width.

NEW WORDS
✎ **expand** To become larger.
✎ **scientist** A person who studies the way things work.
✎ **supernova** A very old star when it explodes.

red dwarf

yellow star (like the Sun)

blue giant

red supergian

The Universe

Our address in space is "Earth, Solar System, Milky Way Galaxy, Universe." The Universe is the biggest thing there is and includes all the empty parts of space between the stars.

Most scientists think that the Universe began with a Big Bang, which happened billions of years ago. Since then it has been growing bigger and bigger in all directions, creating more and more space.

the Big Bang

clouds of gas

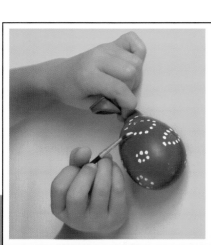

UNIVERSAL BALLOON
Paint white, squiggly, galaxy shapes on a large blue balloon. Let the paint dry, and then slowly blow up the balloon. You will see the galaxies moving apart on the balloon, just as they are doing in the Universe.

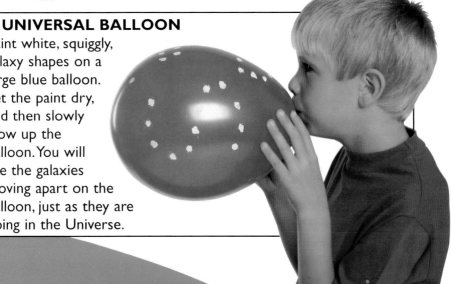

Days and Seasons

As the Earth travels around the Sun, it spins like a top. It turns right around once every 24 hours, and this gives us day and night.

The part of the Earth facing the Sun is in daylight. When that part turns away from the Sun, it gets dark and has nighttime.

We have seasons because the Earth has a tilt, so that north and south are not straight up and down. When the northern half of the Earth is tilted toward the Sun, it is summer there. At that time it is winter in the southern half of the world, because it is tilted away from the Sun's warmth.

March

June

December

September

spring

△ **In June** the northern part of the Earth is tilted toward the Sun. It is summer there then, with long, light days and short, dark nights. In December it is the exact opposite. Then the Sun shines more directly on the southern part and makes it warmer.

🌳 **It takes a year** for the Earth to travel all the way around the Sun. During that time the Earth spins round 365 times, giving that number of days. At the same time the Moon travels around the Earth 12 times, giving that number of months.

NIGHT AND DAY

In a darkened room, shine a flashlight at a globe of the Earth. If you don't have a globe, use a large ball. The globe or ball is the Earth, and your flashlight acts like the Sun as it shines on our planet. The side facing the Sun gets light, so there it is day. On the dark side of the globe it is night. You could slowly spin the Earth around, to see how day and night follow each other around the globe.

In some places around the middle of the Earth, near the equator, there are only two seasons. One part of the year is hot and dry, and the other part is warm and wet.

▽ **The Earth's landscape** changes with the seasons. Many trees grow new leaves in spring. The leaves are green and fully grown in summer. They turn brown and start to fall in autumn. In winter, the trees' branches are bare.

winter

summer

autumn

Looking at the Sky

Since ancient times, people have learned a lot about the Universe by studying the night sky.

Early astronomers simply used their naked eyes. Modern astronomers look through big, powerful telescopes so that they can see planets and stars close up. Today, there is even a telescope out in space, which sends pictures back to Earth.

△ **The sighting of a comet** is an exciting event. Comets are huge snowballs made of ice and dust. When they come close to the Sun, they develop tails of gas and dust that may be many hundreds of thousands of miles or kilometers long.

NEW WORDS

astronomer A person who studies the stars, planets, and space.

observatory A building with a big telescope for looking at the stars and planets.

telescope An instrument you look through to make distant things look bigger.

Astronomers look at the dark night sky. In the daytime, the sky is lit up by the Sun. This strong light makes it impossible to see other stars.

▷ **Big telescopes** are usually housed in observatories. These are dome-shaped buildings, with a roof that can slide open to show part of the sky. The best observatories are on mountain tops, well away from city lights, giving clear views of the sky above.

Copernicus

Galileo

Newton

Hubble

△ **This star map** shows all the stars you can see in a year if you live in the northern half of the world. The stars have been joined together to make constellation patterns. People who live in the southern half of the Earth see different patterns.

△ **Four famous astronomers**. Copernicus was the first to say that the Earth circles the Sun. Galileo designed his own telescope. Newton discovered that the force of gravity keeps the Earth traveling around the Sun. Hubble's telescope showed him that galaxies are moving steadily apart.

▷ **If you are interested** in studying the sky, you could join your local astronomy club.

Traveling in Space

Spacecraft are blasted into space by powerful rockets. Once the rocket has used up its fuel, the spacecraft carries on under its own power.

Astronauts are space travelers. They live and work in space, sometimes for months on end. Astronauts have to do special training, because there is so little gravity in space. This means that everything in a spacecraft floats, including the astronauts.

▷ **A space shuttle** is a reusable spacecraft. It rides on a huge fuel tank to take off, uses its own power in space, and lands back on Earth like a plane. Shuttles are used to take astronauts to a space station.

◁ **In 1969,** American astronauts visited the Moon for the first time. They landed in a lunar module and wore spacesuits to walk on the Moon's surface. The suits protected them, provided them with air to breathe and kept them at the right temperature.

The first living thing to travel in space was a dog named Laika, in 1957. On April 12, 1961, Russian Yuri Gagarin circled the Earth once to become the first person in space. Just a few weeks later, Alan Shepard became the first U.S. astronaut. His space flight lasted just about 15 minutes.

▷ **Astronauts can travel** a short distance away from their spacecraft by putting a special jet-unit on their back. They can move or turn in any direction with this Manned Maneuvering Unit attached to them.

NEW WORDS

astronaut A person who travels in space.

lunar module The part of a spaceship that lands on the Moon.

magnetic Able to stick to metal objects by the power of magnetism.

space station A spaceship in which astronauts can live and work.

What do astronauts eat?
Most space food is dried, to save weight. Water is added to the food packets before they are heated. Astronauts have to hold on to their food, otherwise it just floats around the spacecraft. All knives and forks are magnetic, so that they stick to the meal trays.

The Atmosphere

The Earth is surrounded by a blanket of air, called the atmosphere. Air is very important: without it, there would be no rain—in fact no weather—and no life.

The atmosphere is made up of many gases, including nitrogen and oxygen. We need to breathe oxygen to stay alive. High up in the atmosphere, a gas called ozone provides a barrier to harmful radiation from the Sun.

Mars has an atmosphere a hundred times thinner than Earth's. Mercury has almost no atmosphere at all.

▽ **The higher you go,** the less air there is. This can create problems for mountaineers. When they need to use a lot of energy at great heights, they sometimes wear oxygen masks.

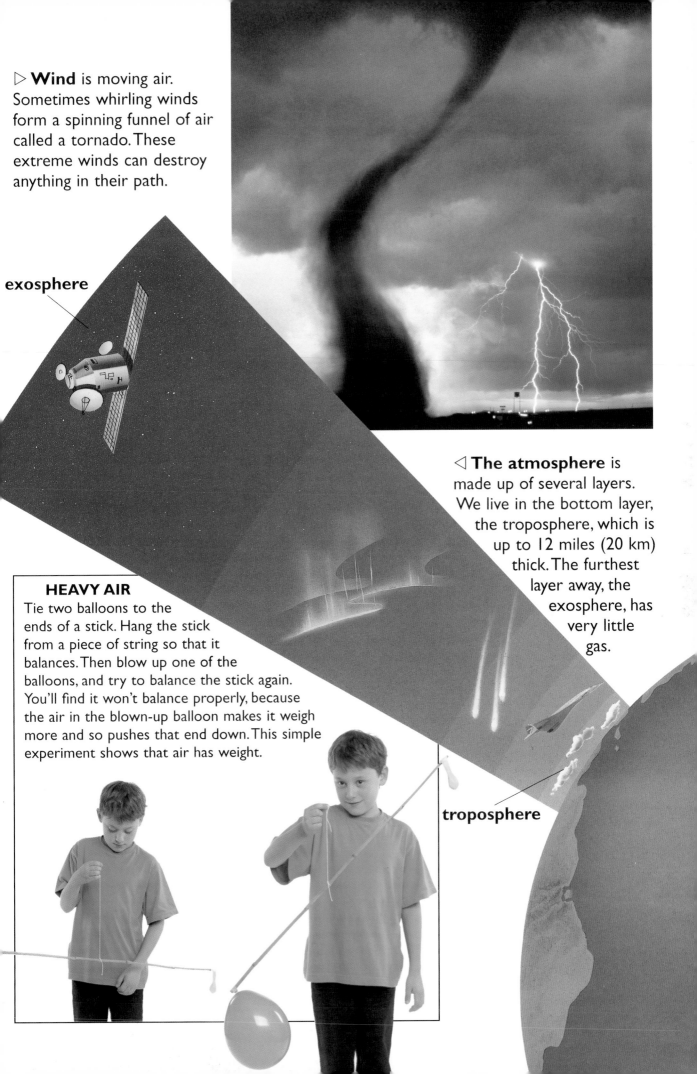

▷ **Wind** is moving air. Sometimes whirling winds form a spinning funnel of air called a tornado. These extreme winds can destroy anything in their path.

exosphere

◁ **The atmosphere** is made up of several layers. We live in the bottom layer, the troposphere, which is up to 12 miles (20 km) thick. The furthest layer away, the exosphere, has very little gas.

HEAVY AIR

Tie two balloons to the ends of a stick. Hang the stick from a piece of string so that it balances. Then blow up one of the balloons, and try to balance the stick again. You'll find it won't balance properly, because the air in the blown-up balloon makes it weigh more and so pushes that end down. This simple experiment shows that air has weight.

troposphere

The Earth's crust is cracked into huge pieces that fit together like a giant jigsaw puzzle. These pieces are called plates. The Earth's oceans and continents are split up by the plates, which float on the mantle.

▽ **Earth** looks cool from space, because of its water. Inside, the center is hot. It is nearly 4,000 miles (6,000 km) from Earth's surface.

PLANET EARTH PUZZLE

Place a piece of tracing paper on the map at the bottom of this page. Trace the thick lines of the plates with a black felt pen, and add the outlines of the continents in pencil. Stick the traced map onto cardboard and color it in. Cut the map up into separate pieces to make your jigsaw puzzle. Jumble up the pieces, then use the plate lines to help you fit your puzzle together again.

NEW WORDS

continent A huge land mass.

core The central part of the Earth.

crust The Earth's outer shell.

mantle A thick layer of hot rock.

molten Melted, or turned into hot liquid.

plate A piece of the Earth's crust.

KEY	
	Eurasian plate
	African plate
	American plate
	Caribbean plate
	Nazca plate
	Pacific plate
	Antarctic plate
	Indian-Australian plate
	Arabian plate

Inside the Earth

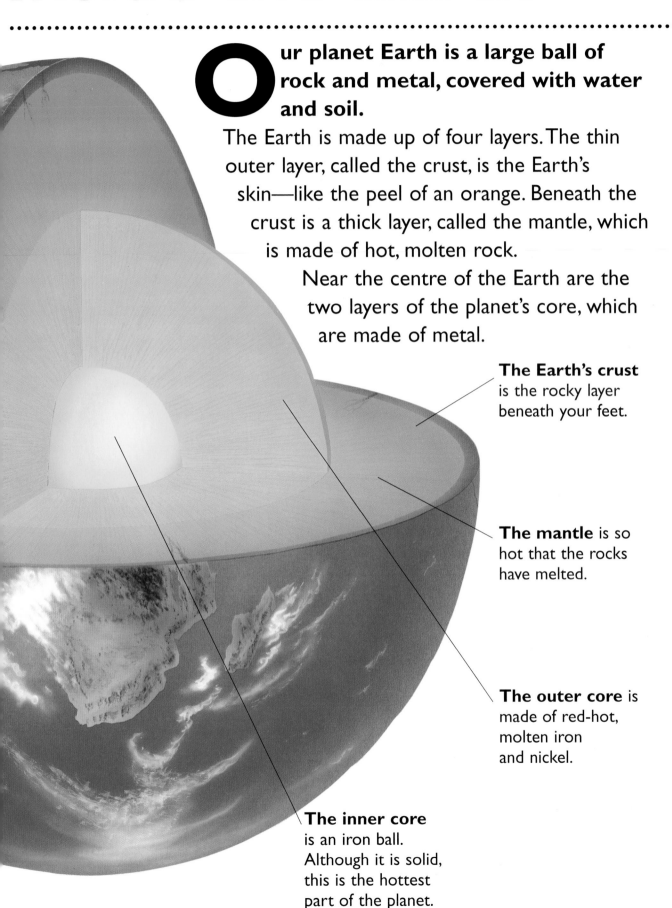

Our planet Earth is a large ball of rock and metal, covered with water and soil.

The Earth is made up of four layers. The thin outer layer, called the crust, is the Earth's skin—like the peel of an orange. Beneath the crust is a thick layer, called the mantle, which is made of hot, molten rock.

Near the centre of the Earth are the two layers of the planet's core, which are made of metal.

The Earth's crust is the rocky layer beneath your feet.

The mantle is so hot that the rocks have melted.

The outer core is made of red-hot, molten iron and nickel.

The inner core is an iron ball. Although it is solid, this is the hottest part of the planet.

Volcanoes and Earthquakes

The plates that make up the Earth's crust slowly move and rub against each other. Though they only move a few inches each year, their buckling can cause volcanoes and earthquakes.

△ **The San Andreas Fault**, in California, shows where two of the Earth's plates slide past each other. They move about 2 inches (5 cm) a year.

Volcanoes and earthquakes usually form near the edge of plates. Many of them happen in a region around the Pacific Ocean called the "Ring of Fire." They sometimes cause giant waves called tsunamis.

The strongest recorded earthquake happened in Ecuador in 1906. It measured 8.6 on the Richter scale, which is used to measure the strength of earthquakes. In 1995, an earthquake at Kobe, in Japan, killed 5,500 people and damaged 190,000 buildings.

◁ **Overpasses and bridges** are at great risk when they are shaken by an earthquake. The quake's waves move out from a point called the epicenter. Very often there are minor tremors before and after a big earthquake.

The world's largest active volcano is Mauna Loa, in Hawaii. It rises to 13,680 feet (4,170 m) above sea level, and is over 30,000 feet (9,000 m) high when measured from the ocean bed. It usually erupts about once every four years.

A volcano that has not erupted for a long time is called dormant, or "sleeping." If a volcano has done nothing at all for thousands of years, it is said to be extinct.

▽ **When a volcano** erupts, red-hot lava blasts up through an opening in the Earth's crust. The steep sides of a volcano mountain are made of layers of hardened lava and ash. These layers build up with each eruption.

NEW WORDS

epicenter The center of an earthquake, where the waves of shaking earth come from.

lava Melted rock that flows from a volcano.

tremor A shaking movement.

tsunami A giant wave that can cause great damage.

Water

Water falls from clouds in the sky in the form of rain, snow, or hail.
When rainwater falls on the land, some of it seeps into the ground and is held in rocks below the surface. In limestone areas, this water makes underground caves. Some water collects in lakes, but most forms rivers that finally find their way to the sea.

water vapor forms clouds

water droplets fall

water evaporates and rises

△ **Water goes round** in a never-ending cycle. First, it evaporates from the oceans. The water vapor rises and turns into clouds. When the droplets in the clouds get too heavy, they fall to land as rain. Some rain flows back to the oceans, and then the water cycle starts all over again.

MEASURING RAIN
To make your own rain gauge, use an empty jar. Pour in a cup of water, 1 tbsp (200 ml). at a time. Use a marker pen to mark tbsp.(10 ml) levels on the jar. Empty the jar and put in a funnel. Then put your gauge outside to catch the rain.

NEW WORDS
cave An underground tunnel.
evaporate To turn into a vapor or gas.
gauge An instrument that measures something.
limestone A soft kind of rock.
mineral A hard substance that is usually found in the ground in rock form.

In caves, minerals in dripping water make stalactites. These hang down from the roof of the cave, while stalagmites grow up from the ground. Sometimes they meet up to form a column.

◁ **Most underground caves** are made by running water. Over many years, rainwater wears away at cracks in soft limestone rocks. The cracks grow wider, making holes and then wide passages. Constantly dripping water creates fantastic rock shapes inside caves.

▷ **Where a river** drops over the edge of a hard rockface, it becomes a waterfall. Victoria Falls plunges 420 feet (130 m) on the Zambezi River in Africa.

▽ **This cross-section** shows how water wears away limestone rocks and hollows out caves. The stream on the surface drops into a sinkhole and forms a shaft.

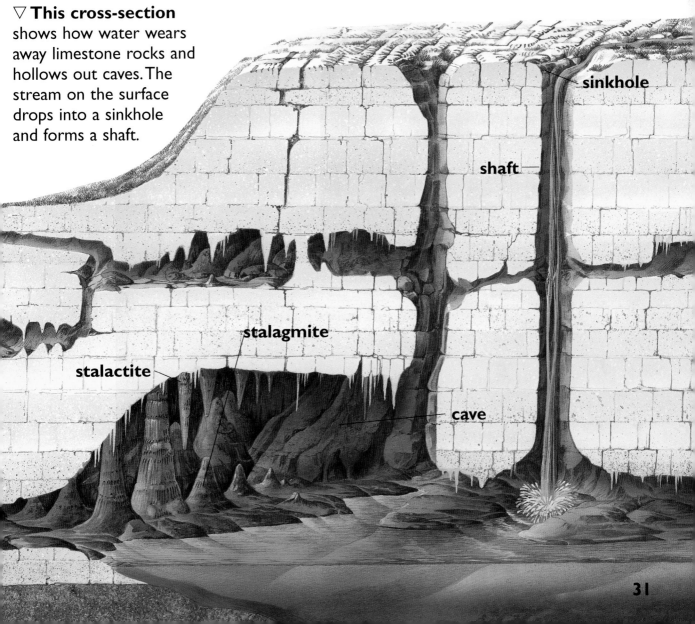

sinkhole

shaft

stalagmite

stalactite

cave

SEA OF ISLANDS
Collect some stones and stick them together with modeling clay. Put your clay mountains in a plastic bowl and pour water in. As the bowl fills with water, islands form. It is easy to see that small islands are really the tops of underwater mountains. How many islands have you made?

△ **Viewed from space**, the Earth looks like a very watery planet. The Pacific Ocean covers almost half the surface of the globe.

The land to the bottom left of the ocean is Australia. At the top left is Russia, and at the top right is the North American continent.

NEW WORDS
coral reef A ridge formed by the skeletons of tiny sea creatures.

globe The round ball shape of the Earth.
trench A valley on the sea bed.

◁ **This sea fan** is a type of coral. Coral reefs usually form in the shallow waters around warm land. They are home to thousands of colorful plants and animals. The biggest coral reef in the world is the Great Barrier Reef, off the coast of Australia.

continental shelf

seamount

trench

guyot

Land and Sea

Millions of years ago, the Earth's land was made up of a single, huge continent. One big, deep ocean covered the rest of the planet.

Over millions of years, the original landmass split itself up into large pieces. As these pieces gradually moved farther apart, the Atlantic, Indian, and Arctic Oceans were formed. Today we call the remains of the huge stretch of water the Pacific Ocean.

200 million years ago

100 million years ago

today

▽ **The ocean floor** has many similar features to dry land. There are mountains called seamounts and guyots, and valleys called trenches. A mid-ocean ridge is where new rock is made from molten rock below.

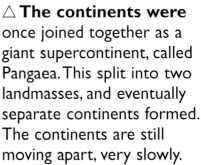 **The continents,** in order of size, are: Asia, Africa, North America, South America, Antarctica, Europe, and Australasia. Together, they cover less of the Earth's surface than the Pacific Ocean.

△ **The continents were** once joined together as a giant supercontinent, called Pangaea. This split into two landmasses, and eventually separate continents formed. The continents are still moving apart, very slowly.

mid-ocean ridge

At the Seashore

Where an ocean meets land, waves pound against the shore. This wears away at the rocks, in a process called erosion.

Oceans carve the shapes of the world's coastlines. Cliffs of soft rock, such as white chalk, are worn away more quickly than hard rock. Waves grind rocks down into pebbles and sand, and they move about as waves break on the seashore.

Twice a day, the water in oceans rises and goes down again. The tides are caused by the pull from the gravity of the Moon and the Sun.

NEW WORDS
☆**erosion** Wearing something away.
☆**pinnacle** A pointed pillar or peak.
☆**shellfish** A type of sea creature that has a shell to live in.
☆**tide** The rise and fall in the level of the sea that happens twice a day.

spider conch

▽ **Coasts** sometimes wear away to make strange shapes. As the oceans break down a cliff face, rocky pinnacles may be left. As they wear away further, the pinnacles eventually collapse.

screw shell

strawberry top

giant clam

punctate maurea

△ **On rocky shores,** shellfish hide in their shells until the tide rolls in. The giant clam has the largest shell. It can grow up to 5 feet (1.5 m) across.

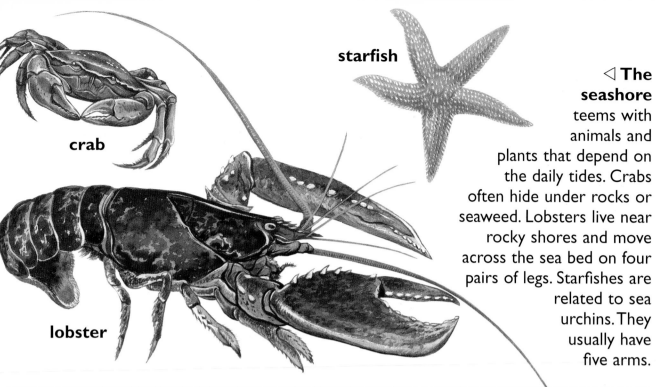

crab

starfish

lobster

◁ **The seashore** teems with animals and plants that depend on the daily tides. Crabs often hide under rocks or seaweed. Lobsters live near rocky shores and move across the sea bed on four pairs of legs. Starfishes are related to sea urchins. They usually have five arms.

△ **Beautiful sandy beaches,** like this one on a Caribbean island, are a great favorite with vacationers all over the world. We don't think of these beaches as rocky, but grains of sand are really just very tiny pieces of broken rock and shells. Sand is popular with shellfish and other shore creatures too, because it is easy for them to dig into.

Lugworms make the coiled tubes of sand that we sometimes see on the shore. The worms dig under the beach, eating the sand for the tiny creatures that live in it.

The world's biggest tides are found in the Bay of Fundy, in the Atlantic Ocean off Canada. There is up to 50 feet (15 m) between high and low tide levels.

Why are pebbles smooth?
Big rocks break away from the land and fall into the sea. The rocks break up into smaller pebbles, and these knock against each other. Eventually they are worn smooth by being dragged up and down the shore by waves.

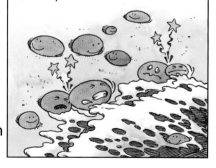

Mountains

There are high mountains all over the world. They took millions of years to form, as the plates that make up the Earth's crust squeezed and buckled.

Mountain ranges that lie near the edge of plates are still being pushed higher. They have steep, rocky peaks. Older ranges that lie further from the plate edges have been worn away over the years by rain, wind, and ice.

It is cold on high mountains, and the peaks have no plants.

NEW WORDS
crag A steep piece of rough rock.
range A group or series of mountains.
strata Layers of rock.

△ **The Earth's plates** are made up of layers of rock, called strata. As the plates move, the strata are bent into folds. In the mountains, you can often see how the layers have been folded into wavy lines.

▷ **The longest** mountain range on land is the Andes, which stretches for over 4,000 miles (7,000 km) down the west coast of South America. The Transantarctic Mountains stretch right across the frozen continent of Antarctica.

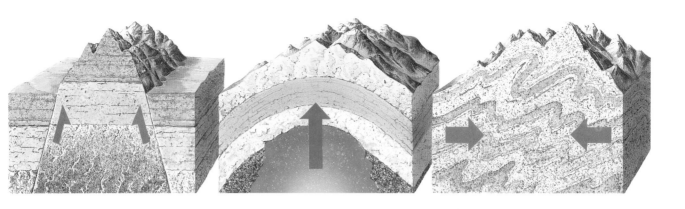

△ **Block mountains** are created when the Earth's crust develops cracks, called faults, and the chunk of land between them is pushed up.

△ **Dome mountains** form when the top layers of the Earth's crust are pushed up by molten rock underneath. This makes a big bulge.

△ **Fold mountains** are formed when one plate bumps and pushes against another. Rock is squeezed up into folds. The Andes were made this way.

Mountains are often joined together in a series, or range. The longest and highest ranges, such as the Andes and the Himalayas, form huge mountain systems. Few animals or people live on the highest mountains.

MOUNTAINS OF JUNK
Crumple newspaper into big balls and tape them onto a cardboard base. Make papier-mâché pulp by soaking newspaper pieces in a bucket of wallpaper paste. Cover the balls with the pulp to make mountains and valleys. When your landscape is dry, paint some snow-capped peaks with white paint. Sprinkle the base with sand. You could add a mountain lake.

What is an ibex?
The ibex is a wild mountain goat that lives in the high mountains in some parts of the world. Ibexes are sure-footed and happy to climb along rocky crags. Male ibexes have long horns, which they sometimes use to fight each other.

The ten highest mountains on land are all in the Himalayas, to the north of India. The highest peak of all, Mount Everest, lies on the border between Nepal and Tibet. It is 29,028 feet (8,848 m) high and is known to people of Tibet as Chomolongma, or "goddess mother of the world".

37

Rocks and Minerals

△ **White cliffs** are made of chalk. This is a type of sedimentary rock, made from the shells of tiny sea creatures.

The Earth's crust is made up of rocks, and rocks are made of one or more minerals.

There are three main kinds of rock. Sedimentary rock forms when layers of sand, mud, and seashells pile up as a sediment and get squashed together. Metamorphic rock is rock that has been changed by great heat and pressure. And igneous (or "fiery") rock is made when hot, melted rock from inside the Earth cools down and becomes hard.

Many of the Earth's rocks are millions of years old, but new rocks are being created all the time.

NEW WORDS

ammonite A type of shellfish that died out millions of years ago.

fossil The remains of an animal or a plant that are preserved in rock.

sediment Tiny particles that sink to the bottom of the sea and then pile up.

◁ **Marble** is a metamorphic rock that forms when limestone is heated and squeezed. White marble is often used for sculpture.

△ **Granite**, a strong igneous rock, was used to build the Empire State Building in New York.

▽ How do fossils form?

Fossils are the remains of living things, such as shells or sea creatures, preserved naturally in rocks.

MAKE A LEAF FOSSIL

Roll out a layer of clay and press a leaf firmly into it. Then carefully remove the leaf, to leave an imprint. Make a cardboard ring, press it into the clay around the imprint, and pour liquid plaster of Paris over it. When the plaster is dry, take it out, peel off the clay and study your leaf fossil.

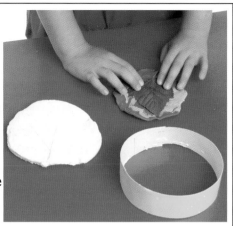

◁ Stage 1

Ammonites were sea creatures that died out about 65 million years ago. When an ammonite died, its body and coiled shell sank to the seabed.

◁ Stage 2

Sediment made of sand and mud fell and built up around the ammonite. The animal's soft parts rotted, leaving just the shell.

Granite is made up

mainly of large grains of quartz, feldspar, and mica. It varies in color from gray to red, depending on the amount of these minerals present.

◁ Stage 3

Over millions of years the heavy sediment hardened into rock and the ammonite's shell was replaced by minerals. This left an outline of the creature's shell inside the rock.

▽ This beautiful mineral

is called selenite. It is a kind of gypsum, which is used to make plaster of Paris, cement, and school chalk.

◁ Stage 4

Today the rock has been worn away by the weather to reveal the fossilized outline of the ammonite. Though this is not the original animal, scientists can learn a lot about the ammonite from this fossil.

northern forest

tempera forest

▷ **The needle-leaved trees** of northern forests are called conifers. They bear their seeds in cones. Trees such as fir, pine, spruce, and larch have to survive long, cold winters there.

▽ **The massive sequoia trees** in California are evergreen conifers, and some are thousands of years old. The largest is nearly 300 feet (90 m) tall, with a diameter of 36 feet (11 m). Imagine trying to climb to the top!

▷ **Ash, beech, maple and oak trees** all grow in temperate forests. In the autumn, their leaves turn brown. Then they shed their leaves to save water and help them get through the winter.

Forests

oak leaf

Almost a third of the Earth's land surface is covered with forests. The trees that grow in forests vary according to the region's climate—how warm it is, how long the winter lasts, and how much rain falls in that region.

Cool northern forests are full of evergreen trees. Temperate forests have deciduous trees that lose their leaves in winter. And tropical rain forests have an enormous variety of big, fast-growing trees.

NEW WORDS

climate The weather conditions of an area.

conifer A tree that makes its seeds in cones.

deciduous tree A tree that loses its leaves in the autumn.

ever-green tree A tree that keeps its leaves.

▽ **Rain forests** grow on warm, wet lowlands. Most rain forest trees are evergreen. It rains almost every day in a rain forest.

The taiga is the world's largest forest, stretching 6,000 miles (10,000 km) across northern Russia. The taiga is very cold during the long, dark winters, and summer in the forest is short and cool.

Millions of creatures live in rain forests, as there is plenty of warmth, water, and food. In the tropical rain forests there are parrots and toucans, monkeys and jaguars, frogs and snakes.

The Amazon rain forest is the biggest in the world. Parts are being cut down at an alarming rate.

rain forest

Deserts

scorpion

NEW WORDS

cactus A fleshy, spiny plant that can store water.
dune A hill of sand.
oasis A place in the desert where there is water and plants can grow.
plain An area of flat country.

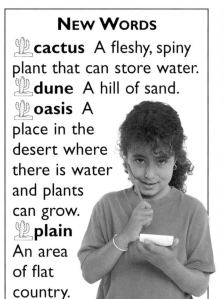

Most deserts are in hot parts of the world, where it is dry nearly all the time.

Some deserts are covered with huge, high sand dunes. But there are many other desert landscapes, including rocky hills and stony plains. In the world's largest desert, the Sahara in northern Africa, the temperature often reaches 120°F (49°C). Despite the heat and lack of water, these are not empty wastelands. Plants such as the cactus and animals such as the scorpion, and even some people, have become used to life in the desert.

Most deserts have small areas of water, where plants can grow and people can live. They are called oases. The Sahara has about 90 large oases.

▽ **In many desert regions**, rocks have been worn away over millions of years by the effects of heat and wind. The deserts of North America are full of strange-shaped, dramatic rock forms.

BAKING DESERT

Mix smooth dough from 6 cups of flour, 3 cups of salt, 6 tablespoons of cooking oil and water. Roll the dough and shape it into a desert landscape. Bake the desert at the bottom of the oven at a low temperature for 40 minutes. When it has cooled down, paint with glue and sprinkle with sand. Paint a green oasis, and add tissue-paper palm trees and, perhaps, a clay camel for effect.

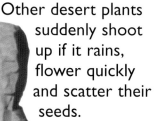

△ **Some of the Sahara's** sand dunes are up to 1,500 feet (450 m) high. They are like seas of sand, and they change and drift with the action of the wind.

▷ **Cactus plants** store water in their fleshy stems. The giant saguaro cactus can grow over 55 feet (16 m) tall. Other desert plants suddenly shoot up if it rains, flower quickly and scatter their seeds.

Polar Regions

▽ **There are icebergs** in the cold sea near both Poles. They are huge chunks of floating freshwater ice that break off from glaciers and ice shelves. Only about a seventh of an iceberg appears above the water, so they are much bigger than they look.

Near the North and South Poles, at the very top and bottom of the world, it is very cold.

The region around the North Pole is called the Arctic. This is a huge area of frozen sea. The Arctic Ocean is covered in thick ice, which spreads over a wider area in winter. Some Arctic people, such as the Inuit and the Lapps, live on frozen land in the north of Asia, Europe, and North America.

The South Pole is on the frozen land of Antarctica, which is renowned as the coldest continent on Earth.

The largest iceberg ever seen was about 200 miles (300 km) long and 65 miles (100 km) wide. It was in the South Pacific Ocean.

◁ **Norwegian explorer Roald Amundsen** was first to reach the South Pole, in 1911. British explorer Robert Scott arrived a few weeks later, to find the Norwegian flag already flying there. At the South Pole, every way you look is north.

NEW WORDS
crevasse A deep crack in ice.
glacier A river of ice that moves very slowly.
iceberg A huge chunk of ice floating in the sea.
treaty A special, signed agreement between countries.

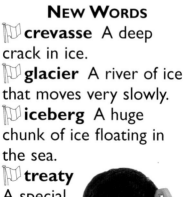

◁ **A glacier** is a mass of ice that moves slowly down a mountain like a river. As a glacier flows downhill, it often cracks into deep openings called crevasses.

In Antarctica, Lambert Glacier flows into an ice shelf, and altogether is over 400 miles (650 km) long. Antarctica's Ross Ice Shelf is the world's largest sheet of floating ice. It is about as big as France!

▽ Working scientists are the only people who live in Antarctica. They try not to spoil the continent, which is protected by an international treaty. Greenpeace, shown here, keeps a check on this. At a research station at the South Pole scientists learn about living in freezing conditions.

Saving our Planet

Many of the Earth's most beautiful areas are in danger. Oceans, seashores, forests, and other regions are being overused and spoiled by people.

We can do a lot to help. Factories can stop pumping waste gases into the air and liquids into rivers. Most pollution comes from people trying to save money, instead of spending more to keep our planet clean.

△ **Some factories** pump dangerous gases into the air. These often get trapped in the atmosphere. Many scientists believe that this so-called "greenhouse effect" could be making the Earth warmer, having drastic effects on our planet.

In some parts of the world, new sources of energy are being tried out. Solar panels collect energy directly from the Sun. Wind farms use windmill generators to make electricity. The power of the oceans' waves and tides are also being used in the same way.

◁ **Drink cans** may be crushed and recycled to make new cans. This saves energy and materials. Used glass bottles, paper, and clothes can also be collected and recycled.

◁ **Oil spills** from huge tankers can pollute coasts. This is especially harmful to seabirds. They get clogged up with oil and then cannot fly or feed.

▷ **Fumes from factories**, power stations, and car exhausts contain dangerous chemicals. Some rise into clouds and later fall as acid rain. This form of pollution can be very harmful to trees.

▽ **It's good for all** of us to plant new trees. They give out oxygen and so help make the fresh air that we need to breathe.

Leaving the car at home
Most cars run on gasoline, which comes from oil. The world's oil is being used up, and car exhausts cause pollution. People can help the planet by walking and using trains and buses as much as possible.

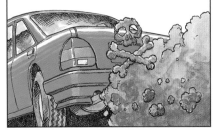

NEW WORDS
🌍 **generator** A machine that makes electricity.
🌍 **pollution** Damage caused by poisonous and harmful substances.
🌍 **recycle** To change waste materials so that they can be used again.
🌍 **solar panel** A metal panel that collects energy from the Sun to make electricity.

Quiz

1. **What is the name** of the planet on which we live? *(page 10)*

2. **What is a round dent** in a planet's surface called? *(page 11)*

3. **How many planets** travel around the Sun? *(page 12)*

4. **Which planet** is closest to the Sun? *(page 13)*

5. **Why do** stars twinkle? *(page 14)*

6. **The Sun** is just one of thousands of millions of stars in our galaxy. What is the name of our galaxy? *(page 15)*

7. **Is our Sun** the hottest star in the Universe? *(page 16)*

8. **Most scientists think** the Universe began with a sort of explosion. What do we call it? *(page 17)*

9. **When a part of the Earth** is tilted toward the Sun, is it summer or winter there? *(page 18)*

10. **When do leaves turn brown** and start to fall from the trees? *(page 19)*

11. **What is a building** that houses a big telescope called? *(page 20)*

12. **Can you name** one famous astronomer from the past? *(page 21)*

13. **In which year** did humans first step onto the Moon's surface? *(page 22)*

14. **What was the first living thing** to travel in space? *(page 23)*

15. **What is the name** of the blanket of air around the Earth? *(page 24)*

16. **Is air** weightless? *(page 25)*

17. **The Earth's crust** is cracked into huge pieces that fit together like a giant jigsaw puzzle. What are the pieces called? *(page 26)*

18. **Which layer of the Earth** lies just under the crust? *(page 27)*

19. **Where is the world's largest** active volcano? *(page 28)*

20. **What is** a tsunami? *(page 29)*

21. **Do stalactites or stalagmites** grow from the roof of a cave? *(page 30)*

22. **Are the Victoria Falls** in Africa or Europe? *(page 31)*

23. **Which ocean** covers almost half the globe? *(page 32)*

24. **Which is the largest** of the Earth's continents? *(page 33)*

25. **What is the name** for the rise and fall in the level of the sea? *(page 34)*

26. **How many arms** do starfish usually have? *(page 35)*

27. **Is it hot or cold** on high mountains? *(page 36)*

28. **In which mountain range** are the ten highest mountains in the world? *(page 37)*

29. **What are white cliffs** made of? *(page 38)*

30. **What sort of animal** was an ammonite? *(page 39)*

31. **What sort of trees** are fir, pine, spruce and larch? *(page 40)*

32. **What do we call** the forests that grow on warm, wet lowlands in regions near the equator? *(page 41)*

33. **Most deserts have small areas with water,** where plants can grow. What are these areas called? *(page 42)*

34. **Where do cactus plants** store water? *(page 43)*

35. **Who was the first explorer** to reach the South Pole? *(page 44)*

36. **Where is the world's largest mass** of floating ice? *(page 45)*

37. **What do solar panels** collect their energy from? *(page 46)*

38. **Why is it good** to plant new trees? *(page 47)*

Science

Science is an exciting way of finding out about the world around us. What are things made of? How can we measure time? How do things work and why do they work the way they do?

Scientists have been asking and trying to answer fascinating questions such as these and many others for thousands of years. They have invented machines to help them and make life easier. In recent times, television and the computer have changed the way many people live and work. Yet plants are just the same as they were centuries ago, and there is still a lot to learn about them, too. Science is knowledge, and science is fun.

Finding Out

The word "science" really means knowledge. It is all about finding things out. We can start finding out by looking at things very carefully. We can look at plants and animals, to see how they grow and change. We can look at rocks and fossils, to see how the Earth developed. We can look at the stars, to find out more about the Universe.

Scientists test things to see how they work. Their tests are called experiments, and they often involve measuring things. Scientists might measure size, weight, or time.

△ **The best way to find out** about an animal and the way it behaves is to watch it carefully for some time. After watching, this boy could look up turtles in an encyclopedia to find out more about them.

▽ **Science** helps our everyday lives. These researchers are using microscopes, computer images, and chemicals to look for new medicines and help fight diseases.

Scientists look through microscopes so that they can see things close up. A microscope can make things look thousands of times bigger, so that you can see tiny details.

When scientists test things, they keep a note of their results. This could be in a notebook, although, today, scientists often use computers to record their information.

Try this simple experiment. Half-fill a measuring cup with water and note down the number of fluid ounces shown on the scale. Then put your hand in the water and see how far the water rises. Again, note down the fluid ounces shown on the jug.
Ask a friend to do the same, and compare your results.

▷ **A magnifying glass** is like a simple microscope. You can use one to see things more clearly and closely. Through his magnifying glass, this boy can see the tiny markings on a caterpillar.

NEW WORDS

🔍**compact disk**
A piece of plastic that carries information for putting in a computer.

🔍**encyclopedia** Books, like this one, or a compact disk containing information.

🔍**microscope**
An instrument that helps you see tiny details close up.

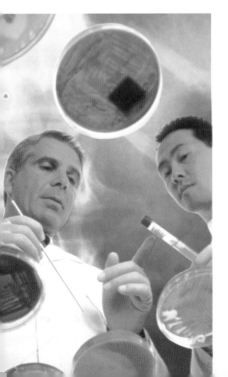

Time

When we are trying to find things out, time is very important. Scientists often need to measure how long it takes for things to happen.

The first clocks and calendars were invented thousands of years ago. They were based on the Earth's movements. We call one spin of the Earth a day. And we call the time it takes for the Earth to travel around the Sun a year. Our time is based on these movements.

▽ **The Earth** is divided into 24 time zones, one for each hour of the day. When it's 7 AM in New York City, USA, it's noon in London, UK, and already 9 PM in Tokyo, Japan.

△ **The sundial** is a type of shadow clock. The pointer's shadow moves around the dial as the Earth spins, pointing to the time. To us, it seems as if the Sun is moving across the sky.

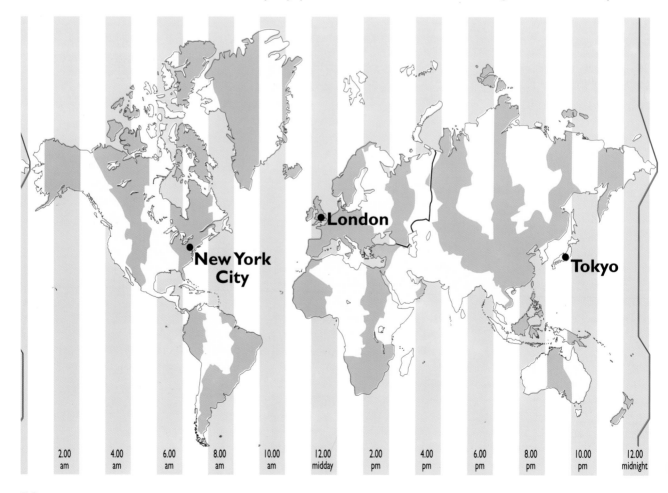

London

New York City

Tokyo

| 2.00 am | 4.00 am | 6.00 am | 8.00 am | 10.00 am | 12.00 midday | 2.00 pm | 4.00 pm | 6.00 pm | 8.00 pm | 10.00 pm | 12.00 midnight |

digital watch

candle clock

grandfather clock

pocket watch

▽ **The Earth** takes a year to travel around the Sun. We split this up into 12 calendar months of, usually, 30 or 31 days.

▽ **The Moon** makes 12 trips around the Earth during a year. These are called lunar months, but do not add up exactly to one year. Muslims follow a lunar month.

WATER CLOCK
Make a small hole in the bottom of a yogurt container. Attach a length of string to the pot and hang it up. Put another yogurt container under it. Then pour water into the hanging pot. Use a watch to time a minute and mark the water level on the bottom pot with a permanent marker. Carry on timing and marking more minutes. Then empty the bottom pot and refill the hanging pot. The marks on your water clock will now show you the passing minutes.

NEW WORDS
🕐 **calendar** A chart that shows us the days, weeks, and months of the year.
🕐 **Muslim** To do with the religion of Muslim people, called Islam.
🕐 **candle clock** A candle marked to show the passing of hours.

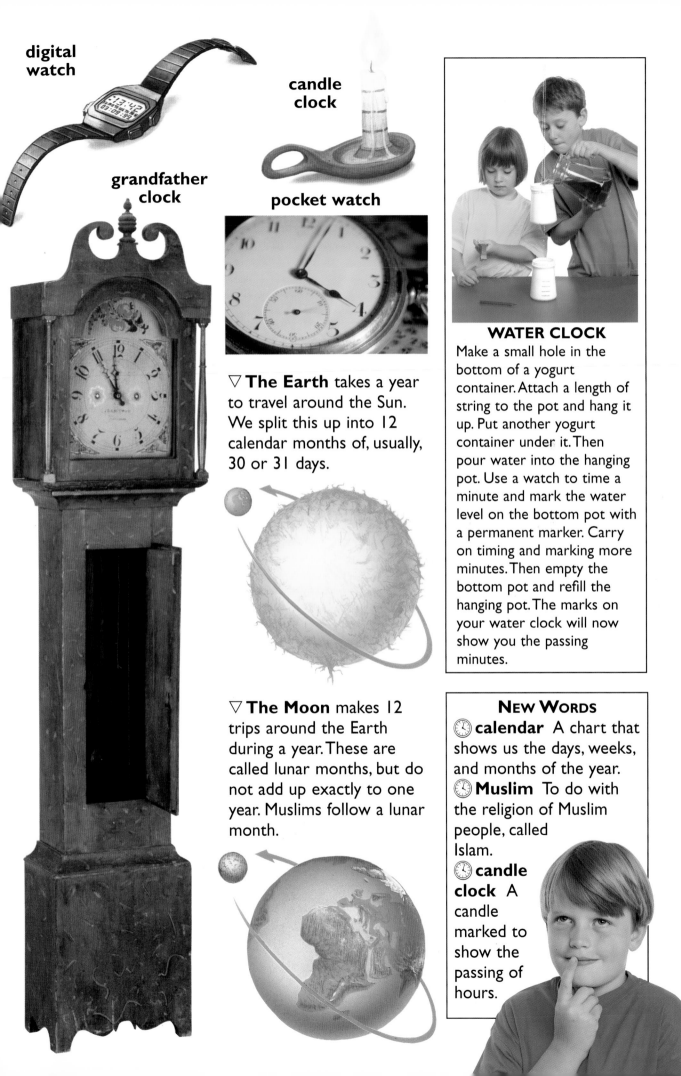

Materials

We use all sorts of materials to make things. Different materials are used to do very different jobs.

Metals are strong and are good at standing heat. Plastics don't break easily and can have lots of different colors. Glass is useful to see through and looks good. Wood has been used by people for thousands of years. Today it is still used to make furniture, as well as paper for books and magazines.

Look around and see how many kinds of material you have in your home.

△ **Wood** can be carved into all sorts of different shapes. It is quite light, but it is also strong. Many things that used to be wood are now made of plastic.

▷ **Many toys** are made of plastic. They are light and don't break or chip easily. This makes them safe for young children to play with.

▽ **Metals** are hard and strong. A hammer would be of no use if it was easily knocked out of shape. Metal can also be sharpened to a point ready for piercing a hole. Safety pins show how useful metal can be.

What if?

In the story of Cinderella, she wears a glass slipper. But imagine really doing that—or trying to bash in nails with a glass hammer! You need to use the right materials for the job.

NEW WORDS

💡 greenhouse A glass building used for growing plants.

💡 plastic A man-made substance that can be molded into a shape.

💡 transparent That can be seen through.

▷ **Glass** is transparent—it lets light through. This makes it useful for drink containers, because you can see what you are drinking. Light bulbs couldn't really be made of anything else!

◁ **The glass walls of a greenhouse** let the Sun's light and heat pass through. This is good for the plants inside. A wooden shed would keep out the light.

💡 **The first plastic** was made by the American inventor John Wesley Hyatt, in 1868. It was called Celluloid. "Plastic" comes from a Greek word meaning "fit for molding."

▷ **Plastics** can be molded into all sorts of shapes. Most plastics will also bend quite easily. Many brushes are made entirely of this material.

Solids, Liquids, and Gases

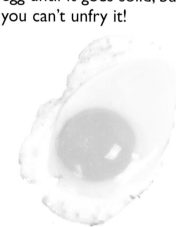

Everything in the Universe, from the tiniest speck of dust to the biggest giant star, is made up of matter. This matter can take one of three forms: solid, liquid, or gas.

A solid is a piece of matter that has a definite shape. Wood is a hard solid, and rubber is a soft solid. A liquid, such as water or lemonade, does not have a definite shape, but takes the shape of its container. A gas, such as air, also has no shape, and spreads out to fill any container it is put in.

△ **When a candle burns,** its solid wax gets hot, melts, and turns to liquid. As it cools, the wax becomes hard and sets again.

▷ **Red-hot lava** comes shooting out of a volcano as a liquid. The lava cools and turns into solid rock. Whether the lava is liquid or solid depends on its temperature. This is the same with candle wax.

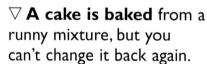

▽ **Concrete** is shaped when it is runny, and then it hardens. A solid concrete building cannot turn into a liquid again.

▽ **A cake is baked** from a runny mixture, but you can't change it back again.

▽ **You can fry** a runny raw egg until it goes solid, but you can't unfry it!

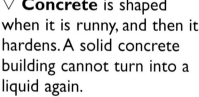

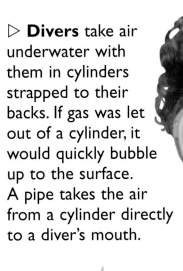

▷ **Divers** take air underwater with them in cylinders strapped to their backs. If gas was let out of a cylinder, it would quickly bubble up to the surface. A pipe takes the air from a cylinder directly to a diver's mouth.

SLOW FREEZER

Salty water does not freeze as easily as fresh water. To test this, dissolve as much salt as you can in a tin-foil container of cold tap water. Then put this in the freezer, along with another container of cold tap water. You will find that the fresh water turns to solid ice much faster than the salty water. This is because the salty water freezes at a much lower temperature.

Can water flow uphill?
No, water always flows downhill. This is because it is pulled by the force of gravity, just like everything else. Water settles at the lowest point it can reach.

NEW WORDS

🕯 **concrete** Cement mixed with sand and gravel, used in building.

🕯 **dissolve** To mix a solid into a liquid so that it becomes part of the liquid.

🕯 **steam** The very hot gas that boiling water turns into.

△ **If you pour water** into an ice cube tray and put it in the freezer, the liquid becomes solid ice. If you then heat the ice cubes, they become liquid again. When the water boils, it turns to a gas called steam. And when the steam cools on a mirror, it changes back to water!

57

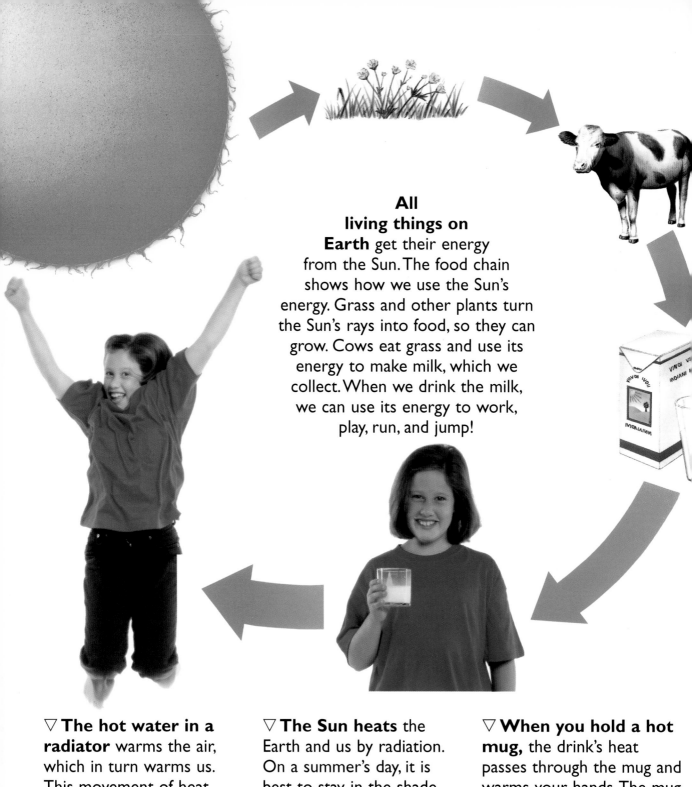

All living things on Earth get their energy from the Sun. The food chain shows how we use the Sun's energy. Grass and other plants turn the Sun's rays into food, so they can grow. Cows eat grass and use its energy to make milk, which we collect. When we drink the milk, we can use its energy to work, play, run, and jump!

▽ **The hot water in a radiator** warms the air, which in turn warms us. This movement of heat energy is called convection.

▽ **The Sun heats** the Earth and us by radiation. On a summer's day, it is best to stay in the shade and drink a lot to stay cool.

▽ **When you hold a hot mug,** the drink's heat passes through the mug and warms your hands. The mug is said to conduct heat.

Energy

All the world's actions and movements are caused by energy. Light, heat, and electricity are all forms of energy. Our human energy comes from food.

Energy exists in many forms, and it always changes from one form to another. A car's energy comes from gasoline. When it is burned in a car, it gives out heat energy. This turns into movement energy to make the car go. Many machines are powered in this way by fuel.

plant and animal remains

oil layer

oil well

NEW WORDS

fuel Stored energy used to power machines.

gasoline A liquid made from crude oil, used to power cars and other machines.

radiator A device in the home that gives off heat. It is often part of a central heating system.

The Sun gives off light energy from 93 million miles (150 million km) away. This is known as solar power. It is the source of all the world's energy, and it can be collected directly by solar panels and turned into electricity.

▷ **Millions of years ago**, the remains of dead sea plants and animals were covered by mud and sand. Heat and pressure turned these into oil, which was trapped between rocks. We drill down to the oil and bring it to the surface. We make gasoline from the oil, which we put into our cars. Then stored energy is turned into movement.

What a shower!

We can save energy in the home by not wasting electricity or gas. Heating water takes up energy, and a shower uses less hot water than a bath. So when we shower, we save energy.

fuel tanker

service station

Electricity

Imagine what life would be like without the form of energy called electricity. You would not be able to make light or heat by flicking on a switch, and most of the machines in your home would not work!

The electricity we use at home is made in power stations. These can be powered by water, nuclear reactors, or fuel like coal, oil, or natural gas. The electricity flows through wires from the power station to our homes. We call this flow an electric current. When you turn on a light switch, a current flows to the bulb and makes it work.

◁ **Another form of electricity** does not flow through wires. It is usually still, or "static." Static electricity from a special generator can make your hair stand on end! You may have noticed this sometimes when your hair is combed quickly, especially on a cold, dry day.

Batteries make and store small amounts of electricity. They are useful because you can carry them around. A car battery is very big. A flashlight battery is smaller. The battery in a watch is tiny.

WARNING!
Never touch or play with plugs, sockets, wires, or any other form of electricity. You will get an electric shock and this could kill you.

60

A flash of lightning makes a booming noise—thunder. We always hear this after we see the flash, because light travels much faster than sound.

An ancient Greek scientist named Thales discovered static electricity over 2,500 years ago, when he rubbed a piece of amber with a cloth.

△ **Lightning** is a form of static electricity. The electricity builds up inside storm clouds, and then jumps from cloud to cloud or from the cloud to the ground as brilliant flashes of lightning.

The American scientist and statesman, Benjamin Franklin, found out in 1752 that lightning is electricity. He did a famous and extremely dangerous experiment by flying a kite into a thunder cloud.

STATIC BALLOONS

Blow up a balloon and rub it up and down on a shirt. The rubbing makes static electricity on the plastic skin of the balloon. Hold the balloon against your clothes and let go. The static electricity will stick it there. You can also use the static to pick up small pieces of tissue paper. What happens when the static charge wears off?

Magnets

Amagnet pulls metal objects such as nails toward itself, with a power called magnetism.

Every magnet has two ends, called its north and south poles. The north pole of one magnet pulls the south pole of another toward it. This is useful in magnetic compasses, which we use to find our way around the world.

The Earth itself is a giant magnet, with strong forces at the two Poles at the top and bottom of the planet. Magnets are very useful in other ways too, from picking up cars to keeping fridge doors closed.

△ **The metal objects** above are all magnetic. If you put a magnet nearby, they would move toward it. Objects made of wood, plastic and other materials are not magnetic. You could collect your own group of small objects and try them out with a magnet.

Make sure that you keep magnets well away from videos, cassette tapes, and computer disks. The effects of magnetism could damage them.

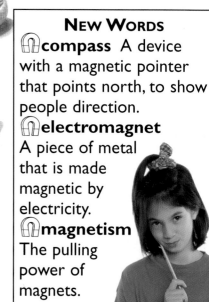

NEW WORDS
compass A device with a magnetic pointer that points north, to show people direction.
electromagnet A piece of metal that is made magnetic by electricity.
magnetism The pulling power of magnets.

◁ **Huge magnets** are used in scrapyards to move chunks of scrap metal around. The crane has an electromagnet, which only works when the electricity is switched on. Whenever the crane driver switches it off, the metal drops from the magnet.

 **When electricity flows** along a wire, it makes the wire magnetic. An electromagnet is made by winding a wire around iron and passing electricity through it. Electromagnets are very powerful magnets.

FLOATING COMPASS

Stroke a needle with a magnet about 50 times. Stroke in the same direction each time, to make the needle magnetic. Then tape the needle to a piece of cork. Float the cork in a bowl of water, and you will see after a while that the needle settles and always points in one direction. This direction is north.

MAGNETIC POLES

Try putting two magnets near each other.

Same poles (north and north, or south and south) will repel each other.

Different poles (north and south) attract each other.

▷ **A compass** helps people find their way. The compass needle is a tiny magnet, and it will always point north, toward North Pole. Line up the needle with the letter N (north) to see where east (E), west (W) and south (S) lie. Compasses are used on ships, planes, and land.

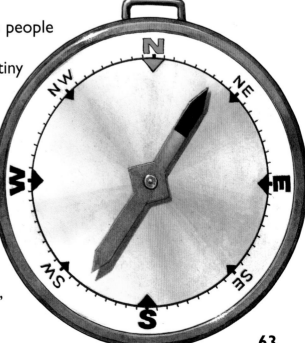

63

Forces

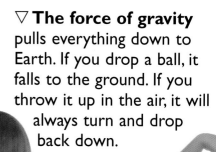

▽ **The force of gravity** pulls everything down to Earth. If you drop a ball, it falls to the ground. If you throw it up in the air, it will always turn and drop back down.

Forces push or pull things. By doing this, they make things move or stop moving.

Forces can make things start or stop, speed up or slow down, change direction, bend or twist. You put a pushing force on the pedals of your bike when you ride it, and the chain and wheels change this force to one that moves the bike along the road.

Everything that moves has a force acting on it. So without forces nothing much would ever happen!

▽ **A tug of war** is a battle of pulling forces between two sets of human muscles. If the pull on one side of the rope is the same as the pull on the other side, no one wins. If one team is able to exert greater force, they will pull the other side toward them.

A force called gravity stops us from floating off the planet into space. It also means people on opposite sides of the Earth all stand the right way up.

pliers

crowbar

△ **A lever** multiplies the force we use to move a weight. A crowbar or pair of pliers works because the farther away from your hands the force is used, the bigger it is.

△▽ **Opposite forces** make boats float. Gravity makes the boat's weight pull it down, but water pushes it up. The weight is spread over a large area, so the water has a lot to push on and holds the boat up.

A rubbing action called friction stops things from sliding. When you pedal your bike, you are working against the friction of the road on your tires. If you ride uphill, you are working against two forces—friction and gravity.

65

SPINNING COLORS
Here's a way to mix the colors of the rainbow back together. Divide a cardboard disk into seven equal sections. Color the sections with the seven colors of the rainbow. Push a sharpened pencil through the middle of the disk and spin it fast on the pencil point. The colors will all mix back to a grayish white.

◁ **Light bounces off** still water in the same way that it bounces back to you from a mirror. The image that we see in the water or in a mirror is called a reflection.

Shadows are dark shapes. They are made when something gets in the way of light and blocks it out. This happens because light travels in straight lines and cannot bend around corners.

NEW WORDS
lens A curved piece of glass or plastic that is used to change the direction of light.
prism A triangular piece of glass that breaks up the colors of light.
reflection The image of something that is seen in a mirror or another reflecting surface.
triangular Having three sides, like a triangle.

In this book, all the colors you see are made of a mixture of just four colored printing inks—blue, red, yellow, and black.

▷ **If you pass a beam of light** through a triangular piece of glass, called a prism, the light gets split up into its different colors, just like a rainbow. The band of rainbow colors is called the spectrum of light.

Light and Color

Light is the fastest moving form of energy. Sunlight travels to Earth through space as light waves. We see things when light reflected from them travels to our eyes.

Light seems to us to be colorless, but really it is a mixture of colors. These are soaked up differently by various objects. A banana lets yellow bounce off it and soaks up the other colors, so the banana looks yellow.

△ **Light normally travels** in straight lines. The plastic lenses in glasses change the direction of light and help people who need them to see things more clearly.

△ **The curved lens** in a magnifying glass also bends light, making things look bigger. You can move the position of the glass, to see things the size you want.

◁ **A rainbow** shows sunlight in seven different colors. This happens when sunlight passes through raindrops and gets split up. Starting with the outer circle, the colors of a rainbow are red, orange, yellow, green, blue, indigo and violet. The colors are always in the same order.

Sound

All sounds are made by things vibrating, or moving backward and forward very quickly. Sounds travel through the air in waves.

Our ears pick up sound waves traveling in the air around us. Sounds can move through other gases too, as well as through liquids and solids. So you can hear sounds when you swim underwater. Astronauts on the Moon, where there is no air, cannot speak to each other directly and have to use radio.

LOUD AND QUIET
Bigger vibrations make bigger sound waves and sound louder. We measure loudness in decibels. Leaves falling gently on the ground might make 10 decibels of noise. A jet plane taking off makes about 120 decibels.

◁ **Sometimes sound waves** bounce back to you off a hard surface. When this happens, the sound makes an echo. A cave or a long corridor are good places to make an echo.

◁ **When you pluck a guitar string,** it vibrates very fast and makes sound waves. If you put your finger gently on a plucked string, you will be able to feel it vibrating. If you press down hard on the string and stop the vibration, you will also stop the sound.

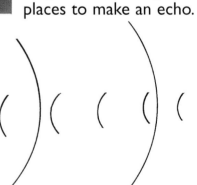

Sound moves at a speed of about 740 mph (1,200 km/h). That's 30 times quicker than the fastest human runner, but almost a million times slower than the speed of light! A Concorde supersonic jet can fly at twice the speed of sound.

HIGH AND LOW

A big horn makes lower sounds than a high-pitched whistle. A big cat makes a booming roar, while a mouse makes a high-pitched squeak. That's because they make different vibrations. The quicker something vibrates, the higher the sound it makes.

whistle

horn

tiger

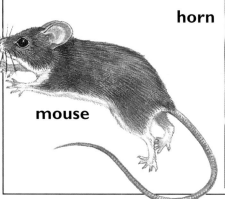
mouse

NEW WORDS

 **decibel** A unit that is used to measure the loudness of sounds.

echo A sound that is heard again when it bounces back off something.

vibrate To move very quickly back and forth.

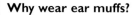 **Dogs** can hear both lower and higher sounds than people can. Bats and dolphins can make and hear even higher-pitched sounds, and they use this ability to find their way around.

Why wear ear muffs?
People who work with loud machines wear muffs to protect their hearing. This is because loud noises are painful to the ears and can damage them, especially if the noise goes on for a long time.

◁ **The vibrations** made by guitar strings travel through the air as sound waves. They do this by making the air vibrate as well. Sometimes people put a hand to their ear to try and collect more sounds.

Cars and Bikes

Today's cars come in all shapes and sizes, from small city cars to big luxury vehicles. Most of them are powered by engines that run on gasoline or diesel oil.

To save energy and cut down on the pollution caused by exhaust fumes, new types of engines are being invented. Cars are also being made safer all the time.

Motorcycles take up less room on the road. Cycles use just human energy to power them along.

▷ **Motorcycle racing** is a popular sport. Riders lean over as they take bends at great speed. This helps them keep their balance and go faster. The fastest motorbikes go at over 180 mph (290 km/h)

▽ **This car** runs on the Sun's energy. Its flat shape helps solar panels to collect the energy. One day cars like this may drive on our roads and highways.

Most cars are built by robots. In the factory, they weld different parts together as car bodies move between them.

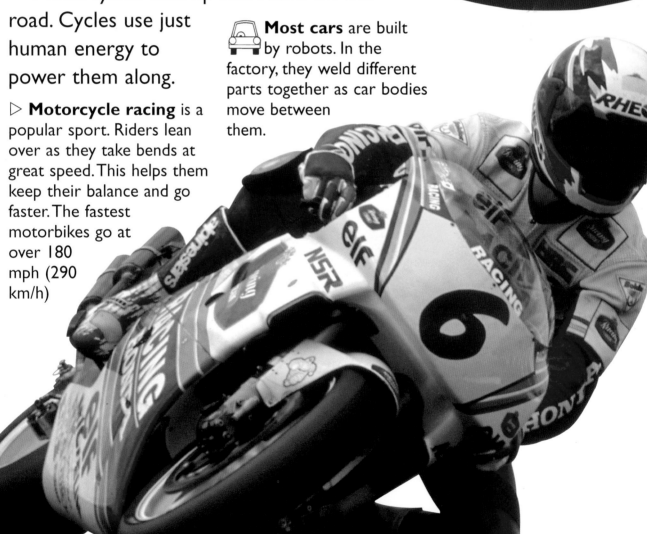

70

seat handlebars

crossbar

brake lever

tire

spoke chain

pedal

NEW WORDS

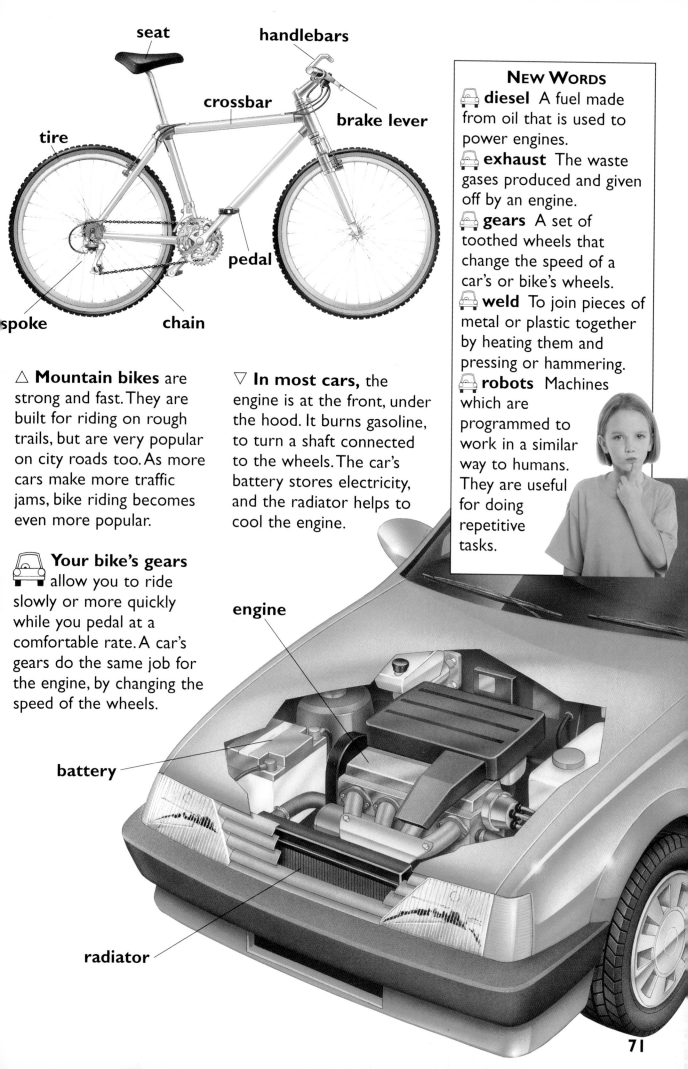 **diesel** A fuel made from oil that is used to power engines.

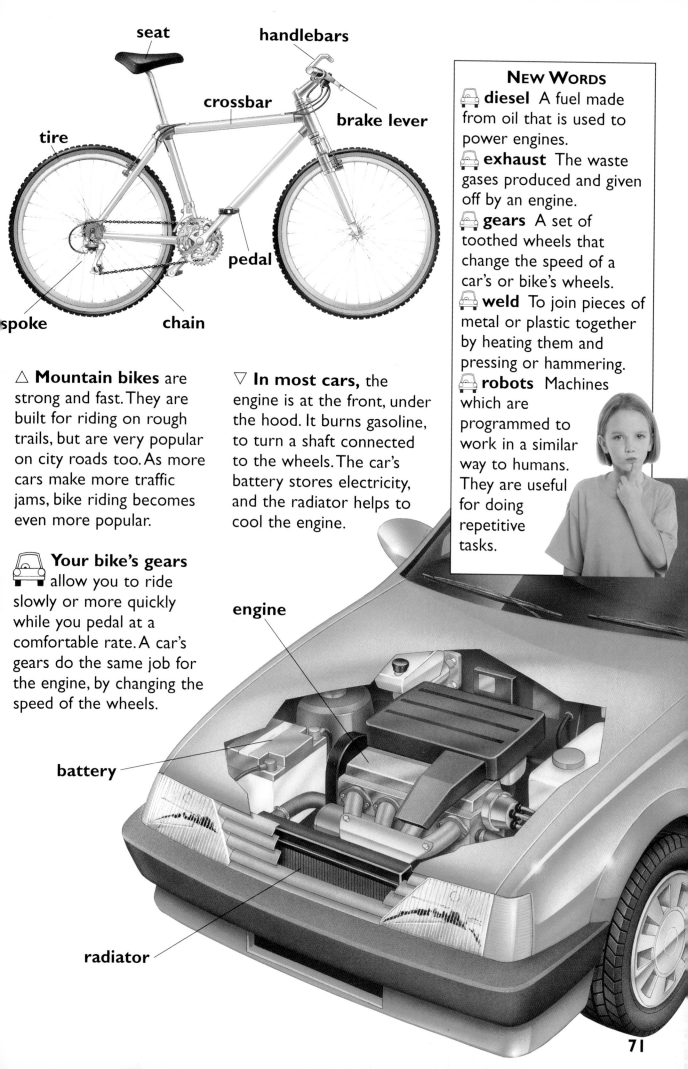 **exhaust** The waste gases produced and given off by an engine.

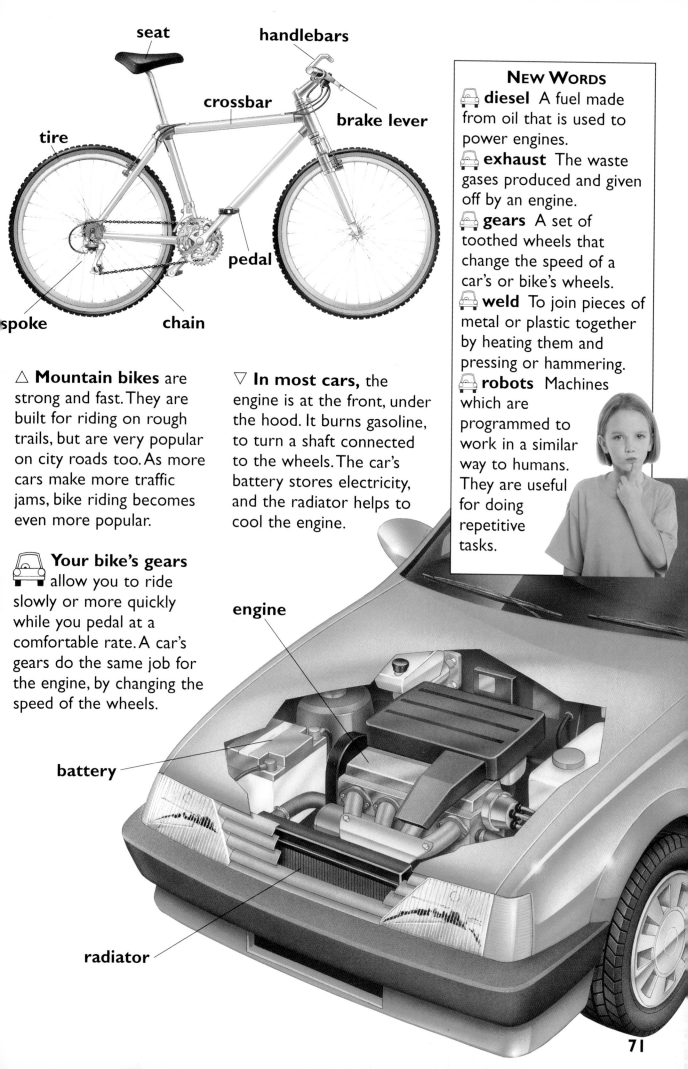 **gears** A set of toothed wheels that change the speed of a car's or bike's wheels.

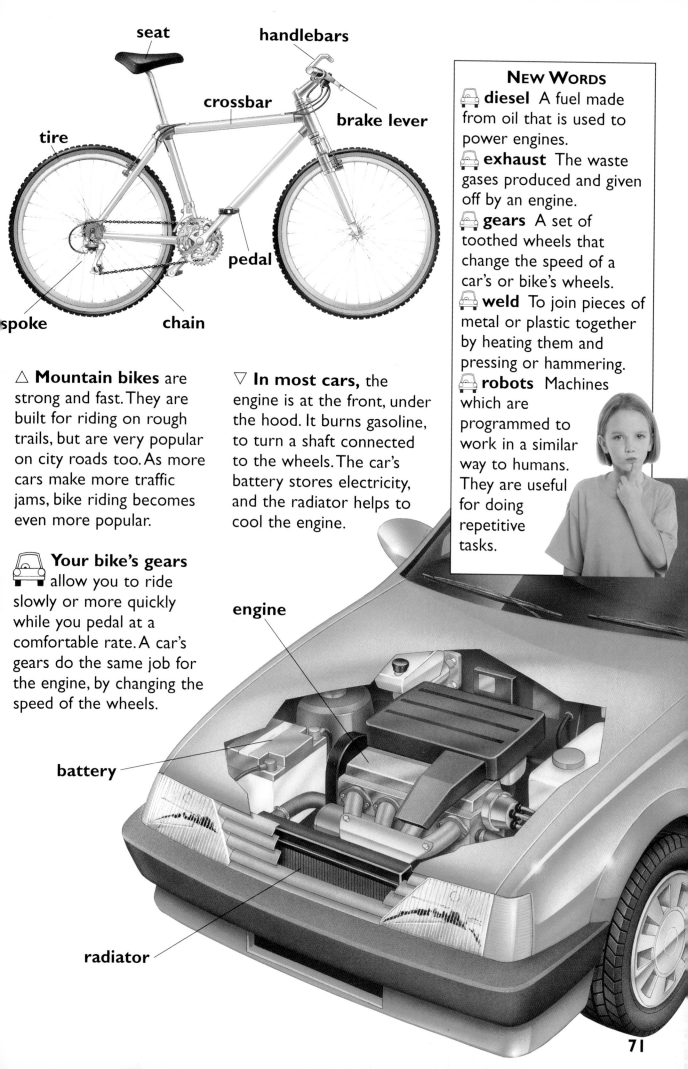 **weld** To join pieces of metal or plastic together by heating them and pressing or hammering.

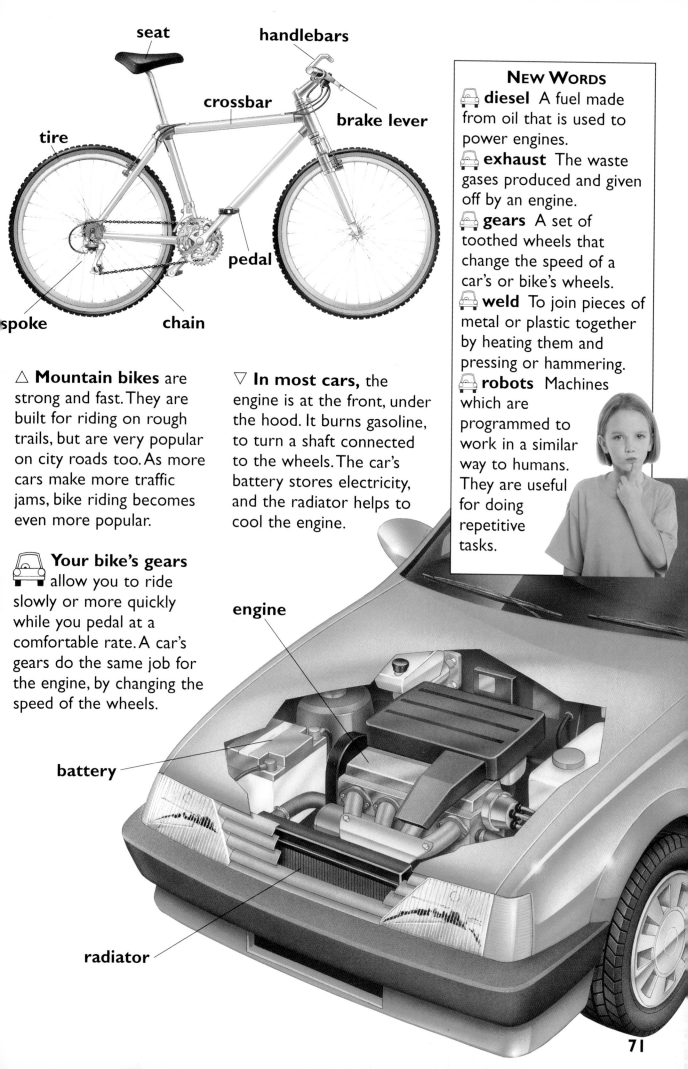 **robots** Machines which are programmed to work in a similar way to humans. They are useful for doing repetitive tasks.

△ **Mountain bikes** are strong and fast. They are built for riding on rough trails, but are very popular on city roads too. As more cars make more traffic jams, bike riding becomes even more popular.

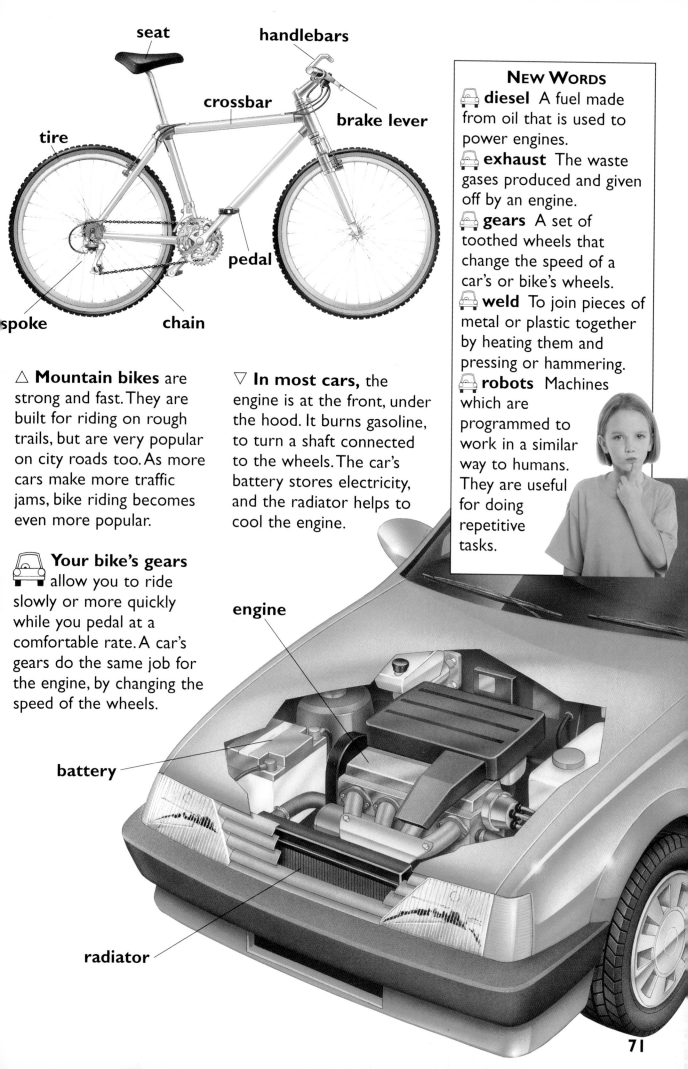 **Your bike's gears** allow you to ride slowly or more quickly while you pedal at a comfortable rate. A car's gears do the same job for the engine, by changing the speed of the wheels.

▽ **In most cars,** the engine is at the front, under the hood. It burns gasoline, to turn a shaft connected to the wheels. The car's battery stores electricity, and the radiator helps to cool the engine.

engine

battery

radiator

Trains, Ships, and Planes

What is a maglev train?
Maglev stands for magnetic levitation. A maglev train floats on a magnetic field and is driven by the effect of magnets. It has no wheels and travels along a guideway instead of on rails. Maglevs may well be the trains of the future.

Some modern ships have water jets instead of propellers to push them along. The jets drive water out at great pressure and can be turned to steer the ship, too.

Trains carry people and goods in railway cars. They are pulled along their tracks by powerful locomotives.

△ **Helicopters** use high-speed spinning blades to fly in any direction. Unlike planes, they can hover in mid-air. They can also land on small helipads on top of tall buildings, lighthouses, or oil rigs out at sea.

Ships have sailed on the world's oceans and seas for thousands of years. Hundreds of years ago they helped people to explore new lands and settle in other parts of the world.

More recently, ships have been overtaken by jet planes as the quickest and least expensive form of long-distance transportation.

◁ **The steam engine "The Rocket"** won a railway competition in 1829. It used coal to heat water and make steam. The steam in its boiler drove two big cylinders, which turned the front wheels.

▷ **Steam locomotives** pulled most trains for 150 years, and some are still running. Railroad designers built long bridges across rivers and valleys, and bored tunnels underground and through mountains.

▷ **Concorde**, the world's only supersonic passenger plane, flies at almost twice the speed of sound, but is noisier than most planes. A Concorde can carry less than a quarter of the number of passengers that a huge jumbo jet can manage.

NEW WORDS

engineer An expert who plans, designs, and helps to build things.

helipad A small landing place specially built for a helicopter.

maglev Magnetic levitation, floating in the air on magnets.

propeller A set of spinning blades that push a ship along through the water.

Oil supertankers are the biggest ships in the world. The largest of all is 1,518 feet (458 m) long.

△ **Some cargo ships** are huge and can carry heavier goods than planes. They often transport the goods in containers that are all the same size.

◁ **Electric trains** collect electricity from an extra rail. This can be on the ground or on overhead cables. New electric trains are more comfortable and quieter than diesel trains.

▷ **In Japan,** millions of people travel on fast "bullet" trains as they speed to work. French high-speed trains, called TGVs, are even faster. They hold the world speed record for trains: 319 mph (515 km/h)!

bullet train

Technology in the Home

Today most people have a lot of helpful machines in their homes. The machines are there to make life easier and to save people time. Most of them are powered by electricity.

Housework is much easier now than it has ever been. Before people had washing machines, they would take hours washing their clothes by hand. Now they just spend a few minutes filling the machine and setting the right wash program.

Home technology means that people have more time—to work or to relax.

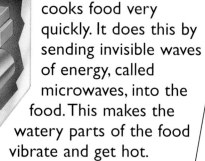

◁ **A microwave oven** cooks food very quickly. It does this by sending invisible waves of energy, called microwaves, into the food. This makes the watery parts of the food vibrate and get hot.

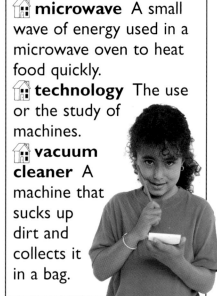

▷ **A washing machine** is really quite a simple electrical device. It works by mixing dirty clothes up with soapy water. A drum inside the machine turns to slosh the clothes in the water, and then clean water rinses away the soap and dirt. Finally, the machine's drum spins very fast, to help dry the clothes.

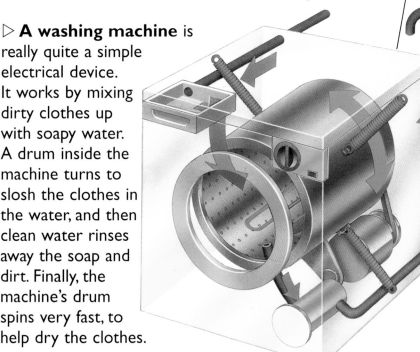

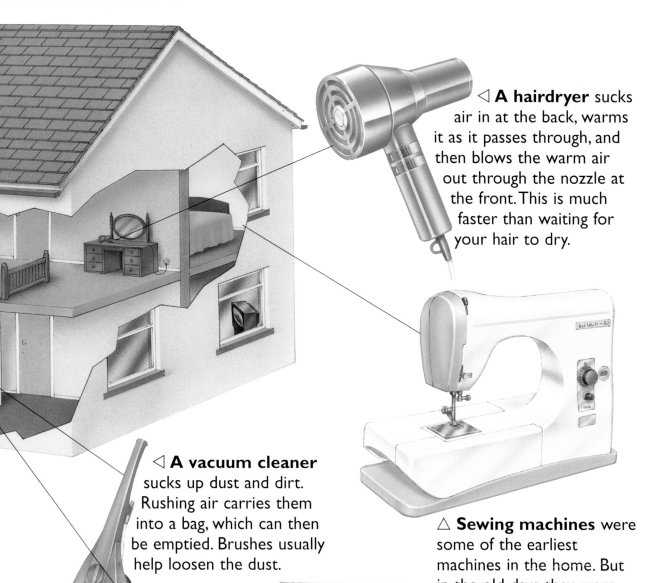

◁ **A hairdryer** sucks air in at the back, warms it as it passes through, and then blows the warm air out through the nozzle at the front. This is much faster than waiting for your hair to dry.

◁ **A vacuum cleaner** sucks up dust and dirt. Rushing air carries them into a bag, which can then be emptied. Brushes usually help loosen the dust.

△ **Sewing machines** were some of the earliest machines in the home. But in the old days they were powered by human effort rather than electricity. The person sewing pushed a pedal back and forth with her feet, to make the needle go up and down. Now an electric motor does all the hard work.

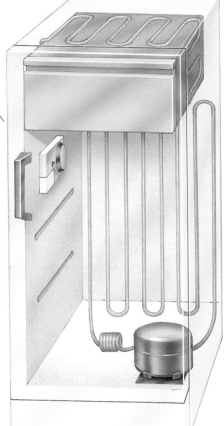

▷ **A refrigerator,** keeps food cold by removing heat from inside the cabinet. A liquid flows around pipes at the back of the refrigerator. The liquid changes to a gas and takes up heat from inside the cabinet. The pipes give off the heat behind the refrigerator.

The first vacuum cleaners were made by the Electric Suction Sweeper Company in 1908. Two years later, the head of the company, William Hoover, renamed it the Hoover Company. In some parts of the world, vacuum cleaners are still called "Hoovers" today.

Computers

Computers can do all sorts of different jobs for us, easily and very quickly. Many people use computers at home, as well as at work and at school.

We can use computers to write letters and reports, store lots of information—such as lists or addresses—do complicated sums, or design things.

Most of the work you do on a computer can be seen on its screen. If you want to, you can also print work out on paper.

▽ **You can use a keyboard** and a mouse to put information into the computer. Then you can store your work on a disk, as well as inside the computer itself.

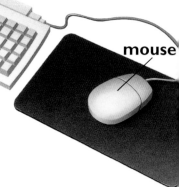

scree

disk drive

keyboard

disks

CD-ROMs

mouse

What is e-mail?

It stands for electronic mail, a way of sending messages between computers all over the world. You write a letter on your computer, then send it down a telephone line to someone else's computer, instantly. In comparison, ordinary post is so slow that e-mailers call it "snail mail."

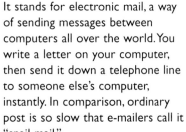

STRINGING ALONG

To make your own phone system, make a hole in the bottom of two plastic or paper cups, or yogurt containers. Then thread a long piece of string through the holes and tie a knot at each end, inside the cup. Ask a friend to pull the string tight and put a cup to his ear. Now speak into your cup and he will hear you. It's as fast as e-mail.

▷ **There are lots** of exciting computer games. You play many of them by using a joystick.

▽ **When you put on** a virtual-reality headset, you enter a pretend world created by a computer.

Inside the headset are two small screens, showing you pictures that look real. If you use a special glove to touch things, the computer reacts to every move you make. This picture shows how the system could be used to control planes. An air traffic controller could see the planes as if they were real and give commands to tell them what to do.

TV and Radio

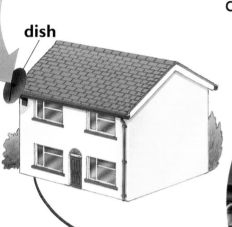

TV studio

satellite

transmitter

dish

pictures are seen in our home

Many people spend hours each day watching TV or listening to the radio. Along with newspapers and magazines, TV and radio provide us with entertainment and information.

Television signals can be received by an antenna or by a satellite dish. Some people have TV signals brought straight into their homes through a cable. In most countries there are many different channels and programs to choose from, day and night.

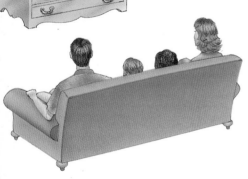

◁ **For satellite TV,** a program is transmitted to a satellite in space. The signal is then beamed back to Earth by the satellite and is picked up by dishes on people's homes. Their television set changes the signal back into pictures.

△ **Working in a TV studio,** camera operators use video cameras to record programs. These are bigger, more complicated versions of the camcorders that people use at home. Many different technicians work in TV and radio.

△ **A TV set** receives electrical signals, which it changes into pictures. It fires streams of particles onto the back of the screen. They build up a picture, and this changes many times each second.

NEW WORDS

aerial A metal device that receives and sends TV and radio signals.

satellite dish A round aerial that receives TV signals bounced back from a satellite in space.

signal A series of radio waves that can make up pictures and sounds.

transmitter A device, usually a tall pole, that sends out radio and television signals.

▽ **South Korea** makes more color television sets than any other country: over 16 million every year!

▽ **A radio telescope** is used to send and receive radio waves. Both radio and TV signals travel as radio waves. Astronomers also use radio telescopes to pick up signals from parts of space that we can't see through other telescopes.

▽ **The largest radio telescope** in the world is at Arecibo, on the Caribbean island of Puerto Rico. The dish is 1,000 feet (305 m) across and stands inside a circle of hills.

▽ **The world's first radio broadcast** was made in the USA in 1906. The first proper TV service began in 1936 in London. At that time there were just 100 television sets in the whole of the UK!

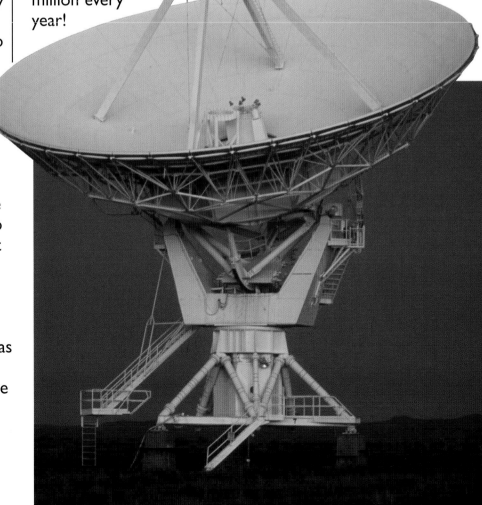

▽ **The leaves** and flowers of water lilies float on the surface of the water. We call these lily pads. The plants' stems are under the water, and their roots are in the mud and soil at the bottom of the pond.

▷ **Some bromeliads** live on other plants, in the rainforest. They grow in pockets of soil that form in the bark of trees. Their roots dangle freely and take in most of their moisture from the damp forest air.

The largest leaves of any plant grow on palm trees on islands in the Indian Ocean. The leaves are up to 65 feet (20 m) long. The pads of some large water lilies grow over 6 feet (2 m) across.

▽ **Leaves** take in carbon dioxide gas through tiny holes on their underside. They also give out oxygen, which is why plants are so important to all other living creatures, including us.

△ **Cacti** live in hot, dry regions, such as deserts. They store water in their fleshy stems. Their leaves are in the shape of sharp spines, which help protect them from desert animals.

NEW WORDS

carbon dioxide
A gas used by plants to make their food; it is also the waste gas that we breathe out.

chlorophyll A green substance in plants, which they use to trap sunlight.

photosynthesis The process that plants use to make food, using sunlight and carbon dioxide and giving off oxygen.

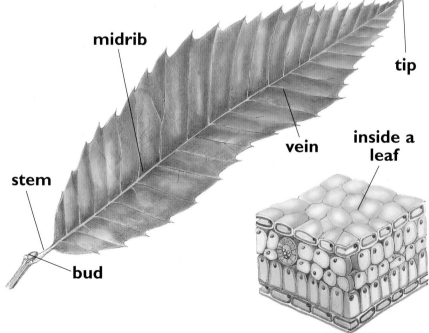

midrib

tip

stem

vein

inside a leaf

bud

Plants

flower

leaf

fruit

stem

roots

Living plants are found almost everywhere on Earth where there is sunlight, warmth and water. They use these to make their own food.

Plants have a special way of using the Sun's energy, with a green substance in their leaves called chlorophyll. They take in a gas called carbon dioxide from the air and mix it with water and minerals from the soil. In this way they make a form of sugar, which is their food. This whole process is called photosynthesis.

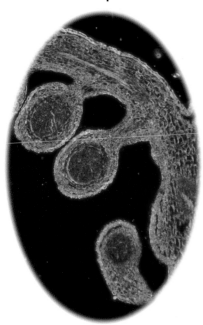

▷ **A plant's roots** grow down into the soil. They are covered in tiny hairs, which take in water and minerals. Water moves through the stem to the leaves, which make the plant's food.

◁ **Part of a fern** seen through a microscope. There are about 10,000 different kinds of ferns in the world. Most of these green plants are quite small.

SUN BLOCK

Cover a patch of green grass with an old can or saucer— but not on someone's prize lawn! Lift the can after a few days and you will see that the grass is losing its color. After a week, it will be very pale. This is because it couldn't make food in the dark. Take the tin away and the grass will soon recover.

Flowers

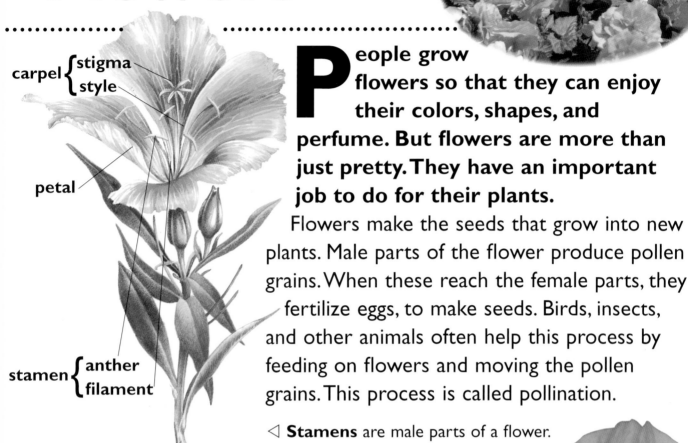

carpel { stigma
style

petal

stamen { anther
filament

People grow flowers so that they can enjoy their colors, shapes, and perfume. But flowers are more than just pretty. They have an important job to do for their plants.

Flowers make the seeds that grow into new plants. Male parts of the flower produce pollen grains. When these reach the female parts, they fertilize eggs, to make seeds. Birds, insects, and other animals often help this process by feeding on flowers and moving the pollen grains. This process is called pollination.

◁ **Stamens** are male parts of a flower. The stigma at the top of the female carpel catches pollen grains, which reach down the style to meet egg cells and make seeds.

△ **A hummingbird** can hover in front of a flower while it feeds on the sweet nectar. Pollen sticks to its long beak and is carried to the female part of the plant or to another plant when the bird next feeds. The same thing happens with bees, when they collect nectar to make honey.

▽ **Some plants** have many small flowers arranged on one stem, while others have one big flower at the top. The petals do not usually last long. Once they have done their job and attracted animals to pollinate the plant, they begin to drop off.

△ **It is easy to see** how beautiful, colorful flowers attract insects and other animals. Many flowers can be found in all sorts of different colors. There are more than 200 different types of chrysanthemums, which are very popular with gardeners.

▽ **There are almost** 20,000 different types of orchid. Some grow on the ground, and others grow on the branches of trees. Their seeds are as light as dust and are known to have been blown over 600 miles (1,000 km) by the wind.

NEW WORDS

carpel The female parts of a flower.

nectar A sweet liquid produced by flowers and collected by bees and other animals for food.

petal The outer, coloured part of a flower.

pollen Powder produced by male parts of a flower, containing male cells for making seeds.

stamen The male part of a flower, where pollen is made.

Bees are the best-known collectors of nectar. They find flowers by their color and their scent. Some bats also feed on nectar, in the same way as hummingbirds. The bats have long, tubelike tongues.

▷ **Some trees**, such as birch and hazel, have flowers that hang down like loose tassels. These flowers, called catkins, often appear before the tree's leaves each spring. The pollen on the catkins is easily blown by the wind, so that it moves from flower to flower and tree to tree.

Trees

Trees are not only among the largest living things on Earth, but also can live the longest.

A trunk is really just a hard, woody stem. Under the protective bark, water and food travel up through the outer layer of wood, called the sapwod, to the tree's crown of branches and leaves.

Fine roots take in the water, but trees have big, strong roots as well. These will help anchor the trees very firmly in the ground.

▽ **Different leaves** do different jobs. Small leaves, like those on fir trees or cacti, lose less water than broad, flat leaves. Big leaves show a larger surface area to the Sun and so are able to make more food.

△ **The beautiful leaves** of the tamarind, an evergreen tree that grows in warm regions of the world. It can grow to a height of 80 feet (24 m)

The oldest living trees on Earth are bristlecone pines in the U.S. Southwest. Some are over 5,000 years old.

Mangrove trees grow in swamps. They are the only trees that live in salty water.

▽ **The leaves of birch trees** are shaped like triangles, with toothed edges. In the autumn, they turn brown before falling from the tree. Native Americans used the bark of birch trees to make canoes.

◁ **As an oak tree grows** and the trunk widens, its bark breaks up into pieces like a jigsaw puzzle. In the middle is a core of dark brown heartwood.

growth ring

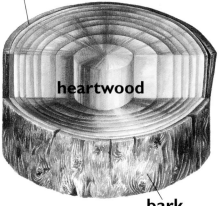

heartwood

bark

△ **Trees grow** a new ring of wood every year. If there is lots of sunshine and rainfall, that year's ring is wide. Foresters count the rings of felled trees to see how old they are.

Many palm trees have no branches. Instead, they have large, fan-shaped leaves that grow straight out from the top of the trunk. Palms grow best in parts of the world where it is warm all year round.

BARK PATTERNS

Every tree has a unique pattern on its bark. You can see these wonderful patterns by transferring them to paper. Just attach or hold a sheet of paper firmly against a tree trunk. Then carefully rub over the paper with a crayon until the bark pattern shows up. Bark rubbings make beautiful pictures, and you can use different colored crayons to make unusual effects.

Fruit, Nuts, and Seeds

A fruit is the part of a plant that protects and feeds new seeds as they grow. **Berries and nuts are really different kinds of fruits.**

Hard shells grow around seeds that will fall to the ground. Soft fruits are often eaten by animals. When a bird eats berries, the seeds usually pass through the bird's digestive system without being harmed. So without knowing it, the bird may later deposit the seeds in ground a long way away.

Some other fruits are very light and are blown by the wind.

△ **Cherries** are small fruits surrounding a hard stone that contains a seed.

△ **The pips in apples** are the seeds. Fleshy fruits are juicy and good to eat. This makes them attractive to animals, which help spread the seeds. We grow apple trees specially for their fruit, and carefully plant the seeds ourselves.

▷ **Nectarines** are a type of peach. Each nectarine has a large, hard seed, which we call the stone. Cherries and plums also have stones.

The world's largest seeds are produced by coco-de-mer trees. Each of the huge heart-shaped seeds can weigh as much as 45 pounds (20 kg).

◁ **It's easy to see** the cluster of seeds inside these juicy melons. Melons are specially grown in warm countries for their fruit.

GROW WATERCRESS

Wild cress grows in streams or on mud. You can easily grow cress seeds yourself in compost, or even on paper! In a tray, place a 1 inch-layer of seed compost, or two sheets of paper towel, and wet this thoroughly. Put the tray on a window sill and always keep it damp. In about 7 to 10 days you will be able to cut your cress and make yourself a tasty sandwich.

▽ **The European hazel tree** grows up to 40 feet (12 m) tall. It flowers in early spring, before the leaves come out, and then produces small, hard hazelnuts.

▷ **Walnut trees** are very useful to people. They give us the wrinkled fruits we call walnuts, and the tree's timber is used for furniture.

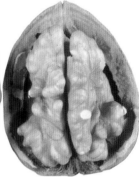

NEW WORDS

digestive system The part of the body through which food passes.

fruit The part of a plant that protects and feeds new seeds as they grow.

shell The hard outer part of a nut.

◁ **Coconuts** are the fruit of the coconut palm. They can float, and so can be carried long distances by the sea, to land and take root on a faraway beach.

The watery liquid inside coconuts is called coconut milk. It makes a refreshing drink.

Quiz

1. What are scientists' tests called? *(page 50)*

2. What can you use to see things more clearly and closer up? *(page 51)*

3. How long does it take for the Earth to travel around the Sun? *(page 52)*

4. How many trips around the Earth does the Moon take in a year? *(page 53)*

5. What material was Cinderella's shoe made of? *(page 54)*

6. Which material comes from a Greek word meaning "fit for molding?" *(page 55)*

7. What does a liquid take the shape of? *(page 56)*

8. What happens to ice cubes when you heat them? *(page 57)*

9. Where do all living things get their energy from? *(page 58)*

10. Which uses less water, a bath or a shower? *(page 59)*

11. Which form of electricity does not flow through wires? *(page 60)*

12. Which comes first, thunder or lightning? *(page 61)*

13. What are the two ends of a magnet called? *(page 62)*

14. Which magnetic instrument helps people find their way? *(page 63)*

15. Which force pulls everything down to Earth? *(page 64)*

16. Which of these is not a lever—crowbar, battery, pliers? *(page 65)*

17. How many sides does a triangle have? *(page 66)*

18. Can you name the colors of the rainbow? *(page 67)*

19. Where are good places to make an echo? *(page 68)*

20. Why do some workmen wear ear muffs? *(page 69)*

21. What do most car engines run on? *(page 70)*

22. What does a car's radiator do? *(page 71)*

23. What does maglev stand for? *(page 72)*

24. What is the name of the world's only supersonic passenger airliner? *(page 73)*

25. What turns inside a washing machine? *(page 74)*

26. Is it quicker to use a hairdryer or to wait for your hair to dry? *(page 75)*

27. What do you store your computer's work on? *(page 76)*

28. In computing, what is a mouse? *(page 77)*

29. How does satellite television work? *(page 78)*

30. Where is the world's largest radio telescope? *(page 79)*

31. What is carbon dioxide? *(page 80)*

32. What is the name of the green substance in plants? *(page 81)*

33. Which birds hover in front of flowers while feeding? *(page 82)*

34. Which insects are the best-known collectors of nectar? *(page 83)*

35. What do a tree's roots do? *(page 84)*

36. Which trees have no branches? *(page 85)*

37. What are apple pips? *(page 86)*

38. What is the hard, outer part of a nut called? *(page 87)*

Human Body

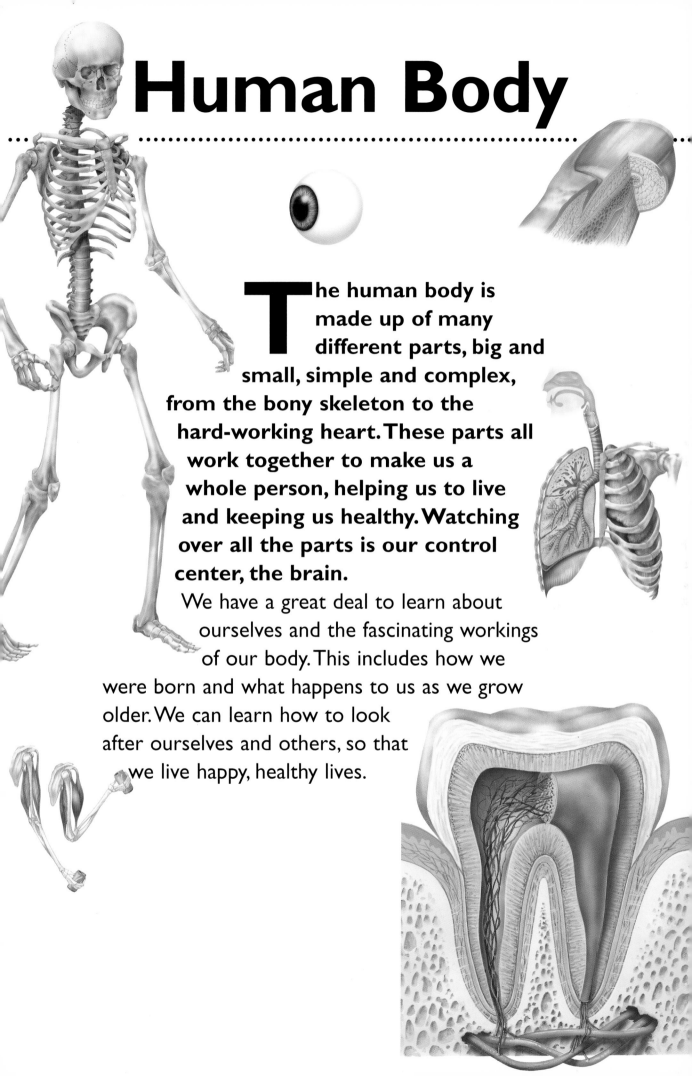

The human body is made up of many different parts, big and small, simple and complex, from the bony skeleton to the hard-working heart. These parts all work together to make us a whole person, helping us to live and keeping us healthy. Watching over all the parts is our control center, the brain.

We have a great deal to learn about ourselves and the fascinating workings of our body. This includes how we were born and what happens to us as we grow older. We can learn how to look after ourselves and others, so that we live happy, healthy lives.

Parts of the Body

head

hand

neck

arm

torso

leg

foot

Men and women, boys and girls are all human beings. **Our bodies are all similar, though no two people look exactly the same.**

The human body is made up of many parts, each having its own special job to do. These different parts are all controlled by the brain, which also enables us to think and move. Our senses of sight, hearing, touch, taste, and smell help us in our daily lives. Our bodies need energy to make it work, which we get from our food.

Two thirds of your body's weight is made up of water. It also contains carbon, calcium, and iron.

◁ **The largest part** of the body is called the torso, or trunk. The four limbs are joined to the torso. The hands at the ends of our arms help us touch and hold things. Our feet help us stand upright and walk. The head is on top of the neck, which can bend and twist. The brain is inside the head.

NEW WORDS

brain The control center of the body, which also lets us think.
limb An arm or a leg.
nucleus The central part of a cell.
tissue Groups of similar cells that are joined together to form parts of the body.
torso The trunk of the human body, from below the neck to the top of the legs.

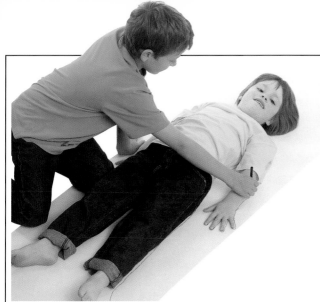

BODY SHAPES
To draw body shapes, you need some very big pieces of paper. Put the paper on the floor and ask a friend to lie on it. Draw around him or her with a pencil. Then take the paper away and cut out the outline shape. You can draw on a face and any other features you want, before pinning the picture up on the wall. Then you could ask a friend to draw your shape.

▷ **All parts of the body** are made up of tiny living units called cells. Every body contains billions of cells, so small that they can only be seen through a microscope. Most cells have three main parts. In the middle is a nucleus, the control center that helps make new cells. This is surrounded by a soft fluid called cytoplasm. The outer surface of the cell is called its membrane.

We all begin life as one single cell. This divides into two, these cells also divide, and so on. Similar types of cells join together to make tissue.

▷ **We have many large organs** inside our bodies. These are parts that do special jobs for the rest of the body. Organs work together to make up different body systems.

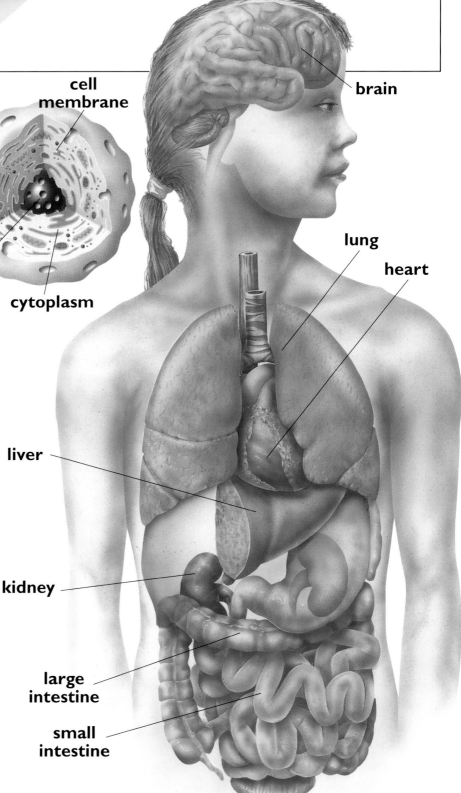

cell membrane

nucleus

cytoplasm

brain

lung

heart

liver

kidney

large intestine

small intestine

Skeleton

he skeleton is our framework of bones. Our bones provide a firm surface for muscles to attach to, helping us to move.

The skeleton also protects our body's organs. The skull protects the brain. Our heart and lungs are protected by the rib cage. The body's bones vary in shape and size. The places where they meet are called joints, which is where muscles move bones.

skull

humer

rib

vertebra

ulna

pelvis

radi

spongy bone   marrow   compact bone

periosteum

◁ **At the center** of bones is soft marrow. This is inside the toughest part, called compact bone, which is lined with spongy bone. A bone's outer layer is called the periosteum.

femur

tibia

fibula

NEW WORDS

joint The place where two bones meet, which allows them to move.
periosteum The outer layer of a bone.
skull The framework of bones of the head.
vertebra One of the separate bones that make up the backbone.

▷ **33 vertebrae** make up our spine, or backbone. At the bottom is the pelvis. A woman's pelvis is wider than a man's, to make room for a baby. The lower parts of our arms and legs have two bones. The femur, or thigh bone, is the largest bone in the body.

MOVING JOINTS

Joints let us move in different ways. The hip and shoulder are ball-and-socket joints. The knee and elbow are hinge joints. There is a pivot joint at the top of the spine, a saddle joint at the thumb's base.

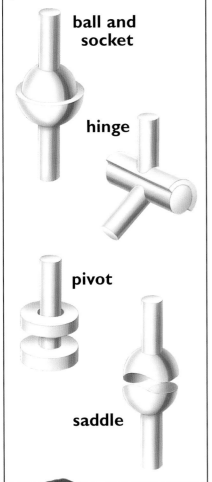

ball and socket

hinge

pivot

saddle

An adult has about 206 bones. Babies are born with as many as 270 small, soft bones. As a child grows, some of the bones join together.

You may be up to half an inch shorter in the evening than early in the morning. The weight of your upper body squashes your spine slightly as you stand and walk during the day.

▽ **For broken bones** to heal properly, they have to be placed next to each other and kept still. That is why a doctor puts a broken arm or leg in a plaster cast. New bone tissue grows to join the broken bone ends together again.

△ **Insects,** such as this beetle, have their skeleton on the outside of their body. It acts like a shell, covering and protecting the soft parts underneath. It also protects the insect from its enemies.

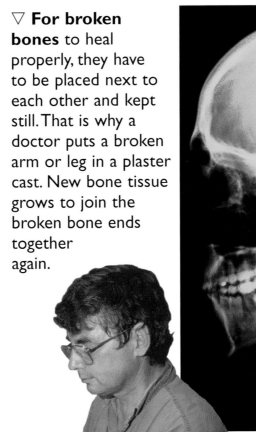

△ **An X-ray photograph** allows doctors to look at bones inside the body. They can then easily see if a bone has been broken or damaged.

Muscles

All our movements, from running and jumping, to blinking and smiling, are made by our muscles. The muscles do this by becoming shorter and pulling the bones to which they are attached.

The human body has about 620 muscles that it uses for movement. In addition there are many more that work automatically. These include the muscles that make the heart beat, the chest muscles that help us breathe, and the stomach muscles that help us digest food.

chest muscles

bice

abdominal muscles

sartorius

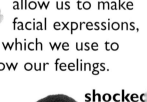

NEW WORDS

buttocks The two rounded parts that form the backside, or bottom.

digest To eat and break down food so that it can provide energy for the body.

rib cage Framework of bones, or ribs, that surrounds the chest.

▷ **The body** is moved by several layers of muscles. There are large muscles near the surface under the skin, and others lie beneath them. Three layers of criss-crossing abdominal muscles connect the rib cage to the pelvis. The body's largest muscle is in the buttock.

▽ **More than 30 small muscles** run from the skull to the skin. These allow us to make facial expressions, which we use to show our feelings.

happy

sad

shocked

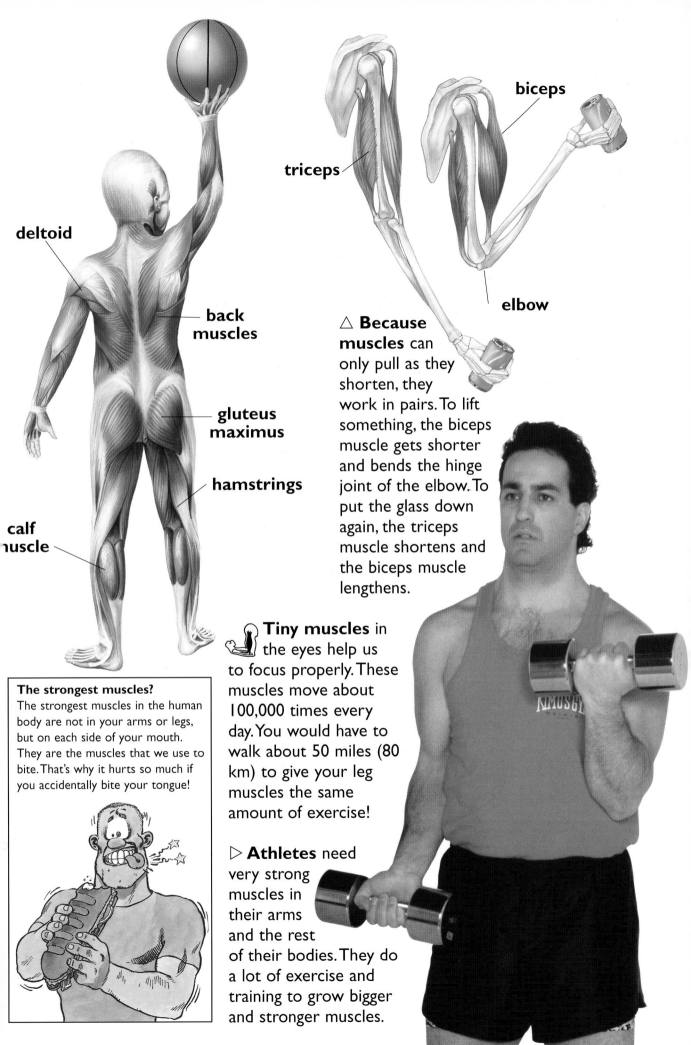

deltoid

back muscles

gluteus maximus

hamstrings

calf muscle

triceps

biceps

elbow

△ **Because muscles** can only pull as they shorten, they work in pairs. To lift something, the biceps muscle gets shorter and bends the hinge joint of the elbow. To put the glass down again, the triceps muscle shortens and the biceps muscle lengthens.

Tiny muscles in the eyes help us to focus properly. These muscles move about 100,000 times every day. You would have to walk about 50 miles (80 km) to give your leg muscles the same amount of exercise!

▷ **Athletes** need very strong muscles in their arms and the rest of their bodies. They do a lot of exercise and training to grow bigger and stronger muscles.

The strongest muscles?
The strongest muscles in the human body are not in your arms or legs, but on each side of your mouth. They are the muscles that we use to bite. That's why it hurts so much if you accidentally bite your tongue!

The Heart and Blood Circulation

The heart is a powerful muscle that pumps blood all around the body. The blood carries oxygen from the air we breathe and goodness from the food we eat.

The heart is pear-shaped and is about as big as your clenched fist. It lies in your chest, behind your ribs and just to the left of the bottom of your breastbone. If you put your hand on your chest near your heart, you can feel it beating. A child's heart rate is about 100 beats a minute. When you are running or if you are very active, your heart beats faster and your body's cells then need more oxygen and food.

heart

artery

vein

Hold one hand up and the other down for one minute.

△ **Blood** travels away from the heart in blood vessels called arteries. It travels back to the heart in veins. In the illustration, arteries are red and veins blue.

▷ **Your heart** has to work harder to pump blood upward, because then it is working against gravity. If you hold one hand up for a minute, you'll see that it has less blood in it afterward than the other hand.

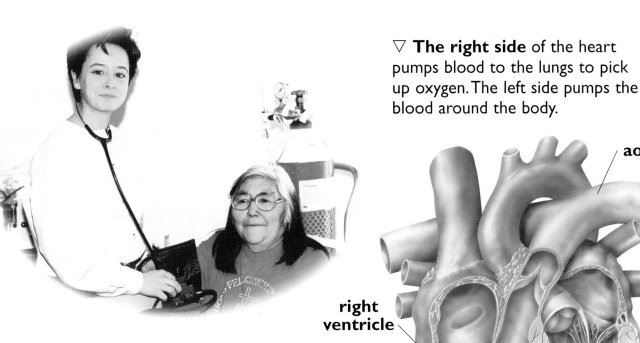

▽ **The right side** of the heart pumps blood to the lungs to pick up oxygen. The left side pumps the blood around the body.

aorta

right ventricle

left ventricle

△ **A doctor** can use a special instrument to measure blood pressure. The instrument squeezes, but it isn't painful. Having high blood pressure can put an extra strain on a person's heart. because it has to work harder.

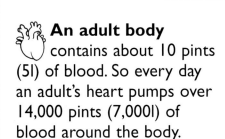

LISTEN TO THE BEAT
You can make your own stethoscope, so that you can easily listen to your own or a friend's heartbeat. Simply cut the top end off two plastic bottles. Then push the ends of some plastic tubing into these two cups. Put one cup over a friend's heart and the other cup over your ear.

An adult body contains about 10 pints (5l) of blood. So every day an adult's heart pumps over 14,000 pints (7,000l) of blood around the body.

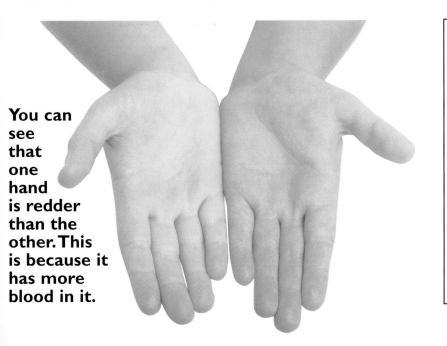

You can see that one hand is redder than the other. This is because it has more blood in it.

New Words
artery One of the tubes that carries blood away from the heart to all parts of the body.
stethoscope A doctor's instrument used for listening to sounds in a person's body.
vein One of the tubes that carries blood to the heart.

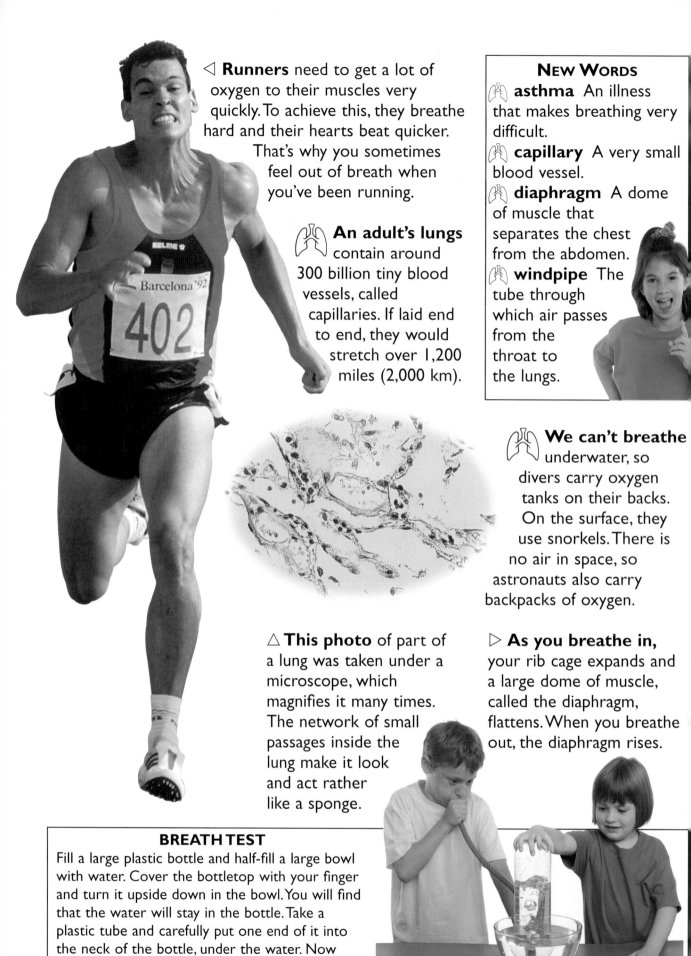

◁ **Runners** need to get a lot of oxygen to their muscles very quickly. To achieve this, they breathe hard and their hearts beat quicker. That's why you sometimes feel out of breath when you've been running.

An adult's lungs contain around 300 billion tiny blood vessels, called capillaries. If laid end to end, they would stretch over 1,200 miles (2,000 km).

We can't breathe underwater, so divers carry oxygen tanks on their backs. On the surface, they use snorkels. There is no air in space, so astronauts also carry backpacks of oxygen.

△ **This photo** of part of a lung was taken under a microscope, which magnifies it many times. The network of small passages inside the lung make it look and act rather like a sponge.

▷ **As you breathe in,** your rib cage expands and a large dome of muscle, called the diaphragm, flattens. When you breathe out, the diaphragm rises.

BREATH TEST

Fill a large plastic bottle and half-fill a large bowl with water. Cover the bottletop with your finger and turn it upside down in the bowl. You will find that the water will stay in the bottle. Take a plastic tube and carefully put one end of it into the neck of the bottle, under the water. Now everything is ready for the breath test. Blow hard into the free end of the tube. How much water can your breath push out of the bottle?

Breathing

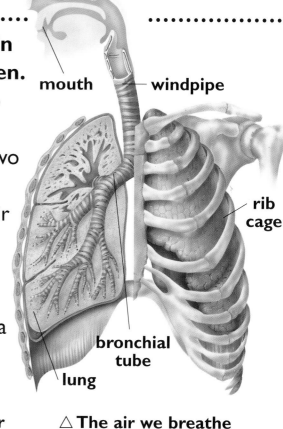

nasal cavity

mouth — windpipe

rib cage

bronchial tube

lung

Every time we breathe, we take in air containing a gas called oxygen. We need oxygen all the time to make our bodies work.

The air we breathe in passes into the two lungs, which are well protected inside the rib cage. The lungs take oxygen from the air and pass it into our bloodstream. Our blood takes oxygen all around the body.

When we breathe out, the lungs get rid of used air. Adults breathe about 18 times a minute, which is more than 25,000 times a day. Children usually breathe even faster.

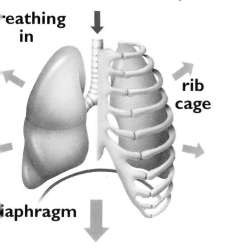

breathing in

rib cage

diaphragm

breathing out

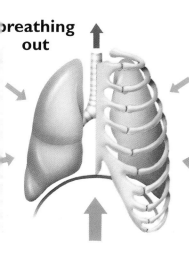

▽ **People who suffer from asthma,** or other breathing difficulties, often use an inhaler to help them breathe. The inhaler puffs a drug down into the windpipe. This makes the air passages wider and they can breathe more easily.

△ **The air we breathe** in through the nose and mouth goes down the windpipe. This branches into two bronchial tubes, one for each lung. Inside the lungs, the tubes divide and get smaller. Oxygen passes from the tiniest tubes to blood vessels and finally into the blood-stream.

Making Sounds

We make sounds when we talk. We can whisper very quietly. We can laugh, scream, and sing. All the sounds that come out of our mouths are made in the throat.

Sounds are made by things vibrating, and your voice comes from vibrating vocal cords. These cords are soft flaps in the larynx, or voice box. They lie across the windpipe, behind the Adam's apple at the front of your throat.

To make loud sounds, we breathe hard over the vocal cords. If you put your hand on your throat and shout, you can feel the vocal cords vibrating.

WHISTLING
When people whistle, they force air through a narrow opening at great speed. The air is squeezed so that it vibrates and makes a high-pitched sound—a whistle.

▽ **Our vocal cords** move to make different sounds. Tiny muscles pull the cords together. When the cords are completely open, air moves freely past them and no sound is made.

closed

open

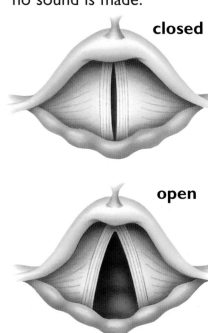

◁ **We use our lips** and tongue to change sounds from our vocal cords and form words. There are a thousand different languages in tropical Africa alone. This Masai man speaks one of them.

NEW WORDS

Adam's apple The lump at the front of the neck.

airway Air passage between the nose and the lungs.

larynx The voice box, containing the vocal cords.

vocal cords Flaps in the throat that can vibrate and then make sounds.

When we cough, we release air at a speed approaching 60 mph (100 kph), trying to remove something that is irritating our airways.

The vocal cords are specially designed to work and make sounds when air passes over them from below. But you can make them work when breathing in too. Try saying "hello" as you breathe in. It's like talking backward!

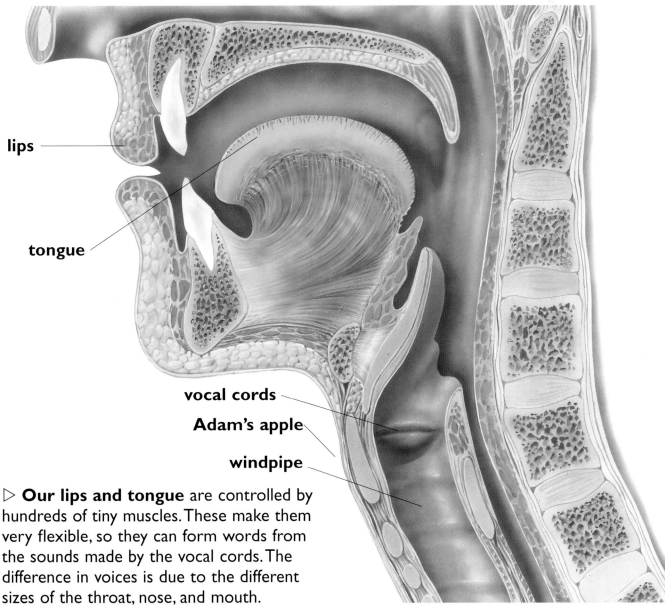

lips

tongue

vocal cords

Adam's apple

windpipe

▷ **Our lips and tongue** are controlled by hundreds of tiny muscles. These make them very flexible, so they can form words from the sounds made by the vocal cords. The difference in voices is due to the different sizes of the throat, nose, and mouth.

Central Nervous System

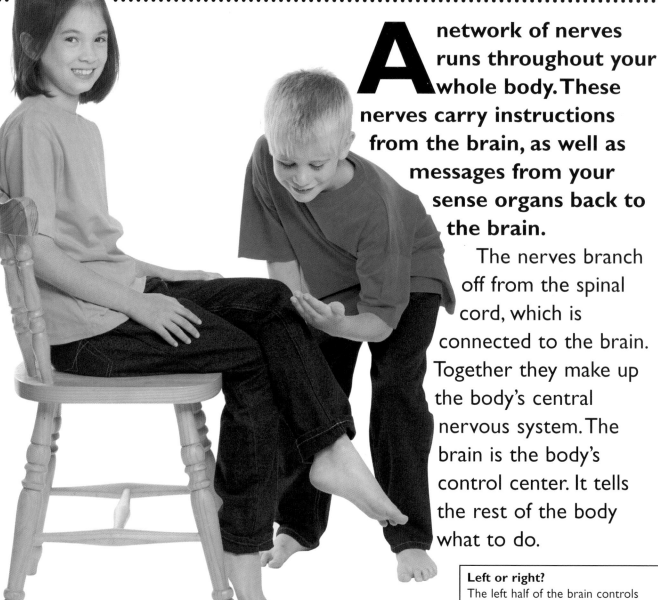

A network of nerves runs throughout your whole body. These nerves carry instructions from the brain, as well as messages from your sense organs back to the brain.

The nerves branch off from the spinal cord, which is connected to the brain. Together they make up the body's central nervous system. The brain is the body's control center. It tells the rest of the body what to do.

△ **If you tap** the right point below someone's knee, his or her leg will jerk. This is called a reflex action. The spinal cord sends a signal back to the leg muscle before the original message has reached the brain.

Reflex actions help the body to protect itself quickly. So if you touch a sharp pin or something hot, you will pull your hand away before the message reaches your brain without thinking about it.

Left or right?
The left half of the brain controls the right side of the body, while the right half looks after the left side. Very few people can write or draw well with both hands. Try using your "wrong" hand, to see how hard it is.

MEMORY TESTER

Put a number of different objects on a tray or on the table. Choose different kinds of things. Then let a friend look at the objects for one minute. How many of the objects can your friend remember with her eyes closed? Now let her put a different set of objects on the table to test your memory.

△ **Memories** are stored in the brain. This couple will always remember their wedding day.

Our brain uses an enormous amount of energy. It uses about a fifth of the oxygen we breathe, as well as a fifth of the energy in the food we eat. With this it produces its own electricity.

▷ **The brain** is connected to the spinal cord that runs down the body inside the backbone. Nerves run from the spine all over the body, even to your little toe.

◁ **Our brain** helps us to see and hear, as well as to judge speed and distance. A racing driver needs to combine all of these abilities very quickly. His brain sends messages to his hands and feet to steer and control the car.

Sleep

Sleeping takes up a lot of our time. Some people need more sleep than others, but most people spend about a third of their lives asleep.

We grow when we are asleep, so babies need at least 18 hours of sleep every day. Most children sleep for about 12 hours each night, and as we grow less, we sleep less. Most adults sleep for between six and nine hours a night. Many old people need very little sleep.

Sleep gives the body time to rest. Our muscles have very little work to do when we are asleep, and so the parts of the brain that control movements can rest too. Our reflexes are still at work, however, so we might brush away a fly in our sleep without even realizing.

We often sleep a lot more than usual when we are ill. We do this to give our body plenty of time to rest and mend itself. When we are well again, we long to get up!

We breathe more slowly when we are asleep, and our heart beats more slowly too. This means that all the different parts of our body are getting lots of rest.

△ **You may think** that you lie perfectly still at night, but you don't. People change their position many times during sleep. This is more restful for the body. If you stayed in one place all the time, your body would ache in the morning.

What is sleepwalking?
Some people sleepwalk: they get up and walk around while they are asleep. They don't know they are doing it, and they usually don't remember anything about it when they wake up the next morning.

NEW WORDS
infectious Quickly spreading to others.
nightmare A frightening dream.
sleepwalk To get out of bed and walk around while you are still asleep.

◁ **The brain** makes a small amount of electricity, and this can be measured by sensors. The patterns are called brain waves, and they show scientists when we are dreaming. As we dream, the brain makes fast, regular waves, like it does when we are awake.

Nightmares are scary dreams. Some people think that nightmares are useful, because they help the brain sort out our real fears and worries. A nightmare might be so scary that it wakes you up. Most people have bad dreams at some time.

△ **Babies** sleep most of the time because their bodies are growing so quickly. If they don't get enough sleep, they cry and are unhappy. Young children need a lot of sleep too.

▷ **We often yawn** when we are tired and want to sleep. But what is it that makes us yawn? It could be that the body needs extra oxygen. A big yawn brings extra oxygen into the lungs. You may feel you want to yawn just looking at this picture, but we do not know why yawning seems to be infectious.

straight hair

wavy hair

curly hair

△ **Hairs** grow from follicles, in the dermis. Different-shaped follicles make people's hair straight, wavy, or curly.

No two fingerprints are the same. Every person in the world has their own special pattern. That's why fingerprints can be used to identify people.

◁ **People sweat** when they are hot, so athletes sweat more on a very hot day. Sweat takes heat from the body and helps cool you down as it dries on your skin.

COMPARE PRINTS

It's best to wear some old clothes and put down lots of newspaper for this activity. It can be a bit messy! Use a roller or a brush to cover your fingers or your whole hand in paint. Then press down firmly on a sheet of paper. This will leave fingerprints and perhaps a whole hand print. When you have finished, compare your prints with a friend's. Are the prints the same? You could try looking at them through a magnifying glass—you'll really see the difference.

The Skin, Hair, and Nails

nail

half-moon

cuticle

skin

fat

bone

Skin protects the body and controls its temperature. It keeps out dirt, water, and germs, shields us from the Sun's burning rays, and stops the body drying out.

△ **Nails** are made of a tough substance called keratin. New nail grows from the base, under the skin. The pale half-moon is nail that has just grown.

Our skin is full of nerve endings, so it can send messages to the brain about things such as heat, cold, and pain. The skin produces nails to protect the tips of fingers and toes. It also makes hairs for extra warmth and protection.

▽ **The tough outer layer** of the skin is called the epidermis, which is waterproof and germproof. The inner layer, called the dermis, contains nerve endings. This is also where hairs grow and sweat is made.

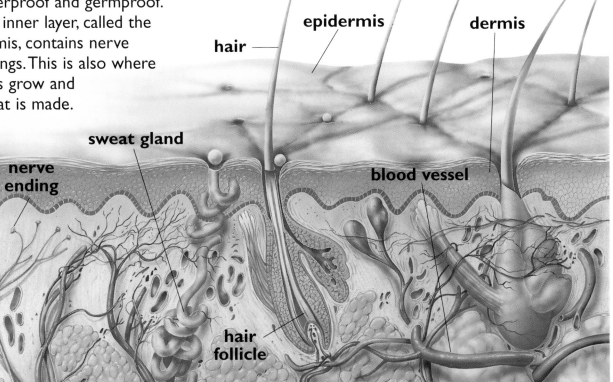

hair

epidermis

dermis

sweat gland

blood vessel

nerve ending

hair follicle

Teeth

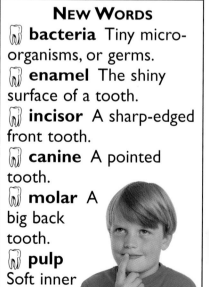

Our teeth are there to break food down into small pieces, ready for swallowing. The teeth have three different shapes, designed to do different jobs.

The incisors at the front are for biting into food and cutting it up. The pointed canines tear tough food. And the big molars at the back grind and mash it.

Children lose their first set of teeth, known as baby, or milk teeth, which start to fall out when we are five or six. A set of new, bigger teeth grows in their place.

▽ **The outside of the tooth** is a hard layer of enamel. The center of the tooth, with blood vessels and nerves, is surrounded by a substance known as dentine.

△ **You should visit** the dentist regularly to have your teeth checked and cleaned. Any tooth decay can be removed and replaced with a filling.

If sugar and bacteria are left on the teeth for long, they can produce acid. This breaks down enamel and causes tooth decay. Regular brushing removes the sugar and bacteria.

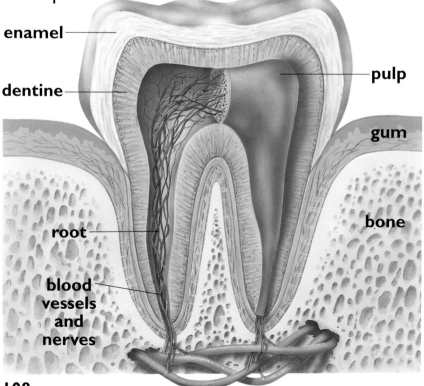

enamel

dentine

pulp

gum

bone

root

blood vessels and nerves

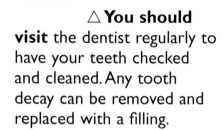

NEW WORDS

bacteria Tiny micro-organisms, or germs.

enamel The shiny surface of a tooth.

incisor A sharp-edged front tooth.

canine A pointed tooth.

molar A big back tooth.

pulp Soft inner tooth.

CHECKING YOUR TEETH

Plaque is a filmy deposit on the surface of teeth that causes decay. You can check how much plaque there is on your teeth by chewing a disclosing tablet (from a drugstore), made of vegetable dye. Plaque shows up as a deep pink color. Brushing your teeth well and regularly will mean less plaque and so less tooth decay.

When old people lose their teeth, they sometimes replace them with false teeth.

▽ **When you are small,** you have 20 baby teeth, shown in the inner circle. These are replaced by 32 permanent teeth, including four back wisdom teeth.

It has been known for people to grow a third set of teeth, but this is very rare indeed.

▽ **It is important** to look after your teeth well when you are a child, so that they will be healthy and strong when you are older. Some children and young adults wear braces for some time. This helps to make crooked teeth straight. Your dentist will tell you if this is a good idea.

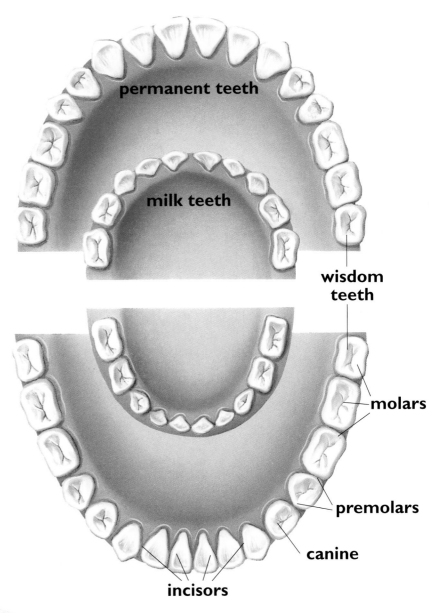

permanent teeth

milk teeth

wisdom teeth

molars

premolars

canine

incisors

△ **The four wisdom teeth** come through last, after the age of about 17. Some people never have wisdom teeth.

Our back teeth grind up our food, which mixes with saliva and goes soft and mushy. This makes it much easier to swallow and digest.

109

Digestion

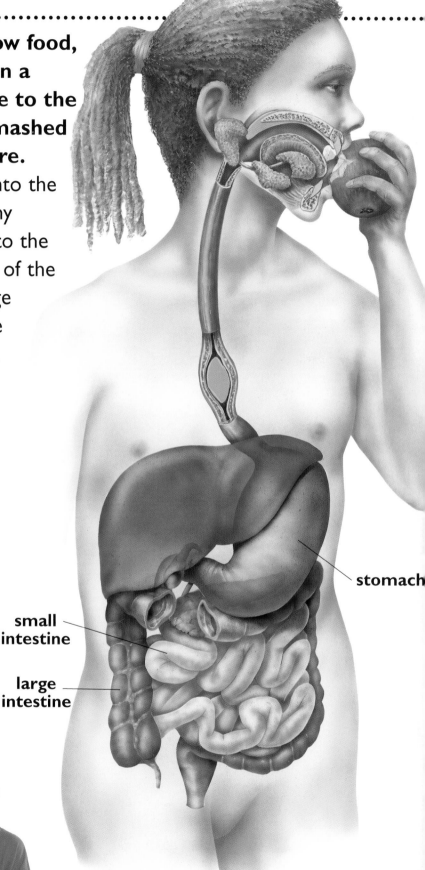

After we swallow food, it travels down a muscular tube to the stomach. There it is mashed into a souplike mixture.

The mixture passes into the small intestine, where tiny particles of food pass into the bloodstream. What's left of the food passes into the large intestine, and then waste products leave the body.

▷ **Digestion** takes up to 18 hours, from biting the apple to tiny particles of it passing into the bloodstream. Food stays in the stomach for three hours.

stomach

small intestine

large intestine

NEW WORDS
🍎 **digestion** The process of breaking food down and passing it into the bloodstream.
🍎 **large intestine** The wide tube where water is removed from the waste products of food.
🍎 **small intestine** The tube where food passes to the bloodstream.
🍎 **villi** Bumps in the small intestine.

> **When we play,** we use up a great deal of energy. We need to eat and digest food to provide our body with that energy.

▽ **In the large intestine,** water is taken out of the parts of food that our body cannot use. The water becomes urine and the rest is solid waste. These pass out of the body when we go to the toilet.

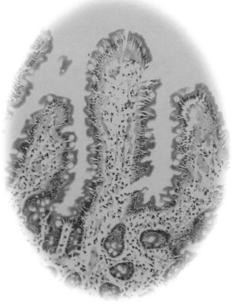

△ **Inside the small intestine** are fingerlike bumps, called villi. These contain blood vessels that take the useful substances from food into our bloodstream. Blood, pumped by the heart, takes the energy from food to all parts of the body.

The small intestine is made up of over 16 feet (5 m) of coiled-up tube. It is longer than the large intestine, but the large intestine is much wider.

111

Food and Drink

We need energy to live, and we get that energy from what we eat and drink. Our bodies need important substances, called nutrients, that we get from food. They help us grow and repair damaged cells, as well as providing energy.

Different foods are useful to us in different ways. It is important that we don't miss out on any of the essential nutrients. To have a balanced diet, we must eat foods from various groups— carbohydrates, proteins, fats, and fiber, also vitamins and minerals.

△ **Cereals and vegetables** are good to eat because they contain a lot of fiber. This is very useful because it helps other foods pass more easily through the digestive system.

The body needs small amounts of minerals, such as calcium and sodium. Calcium is needed for healthy bones and teeth. Milk contains calcium, as well as water, fat, protein, and vitamins.

◁ **Oranges** and other fruit contain a lot of Vitamin C, which keeps us healthy and helps us recover from illness. The body needs many other vitamins too.

▽ **Fats** such as cheese, butter, and milk are full of energy, as well as important vitamins. Fats can be stored by the body to use later, but it is not good to eat too many fatty foods.

△ **Beans and meat** contain lots of proteins, which help us stay strong. They are also used to make body cells, so they help us grow and stay healthy.

▽ **Carbohydrates,** such as bread and pasta, give us a lot of the energy that we need for our daily lives. We can make use of this type of energy very quickly.

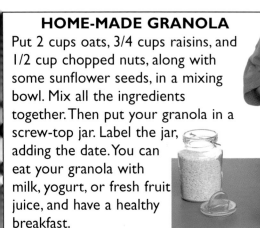

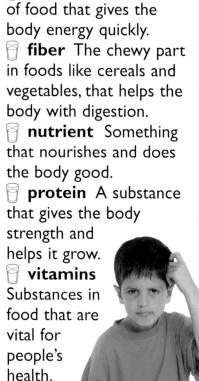

NEW WORDS

carbohydrate A type of food that gives the body energy quickly.

fiber The chewy part in foods like cereals and vegetables, that helps the body with digestion.

nutrient Something that nourishes and does the body good.

protein A substance that gives the body strength and helps it grow.

vitamins Substances in food that are vital for people's health.

Why do we need water?

The body uses water in many ways. Water helps to make up our blood. It keeps us cool by making sweat. It carries wastes from the body in urine. We get water from other drinks too, as well as from many different kinds of food.

HOME-MADE GRANOLA

Put 2 cups oats, 3/4 cups raisins, and 1/2 cup chopped nuts, along with some sunflower seeds, in a mixing bowl. Mix all the ingredients together. Then put your granola in a screw-top jar. Label the jar, adding the date. You can eat your granola with milk, yogurt, or fresh fruit juice, and have a healthy breakfast.

Smell and Taste

Smell and taste are important senses. Our sense of smell is much stronger than our sense of taste. When we taste food, we rely on its smell and texture to give us information about it as well.

We use our noses for smelling things. Tiny scent particles go into the nose with the air. The nose then sends messages through a nerve to the brain, which recognizes the smell.

The tongue also sends nerve signals to the brain about tastes. When we eat something, the tongue and the nose combine to let the brain know all about that particular food.

△ **Flowers** give off a pleasant scent, to attract insects. A skunk can make a very nasty smell when it wants to scare off enemies.

When you have a cold and your nose is plugged, you can't smell much and you can't taste your food properly either.

▷ **We taste different things** on different parts of the tongue. We taste sweet things at the tip, salty things just behind the tip, sour things at the sides, and bitter things at the back of the tongue.

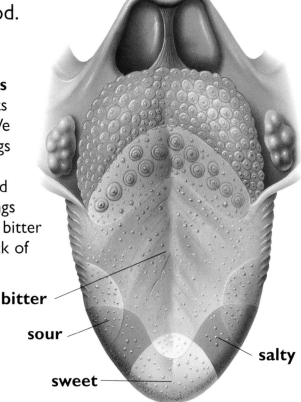

bitter

sour

sweet

salty

Why do we sneeze?
We sneeze to help clear our noses of unwanted particles, such as dust. When we sneeze, the explosive rush of air from the lungs can reach a speed of 100 mph (160 kph)—as fast as a sports car!

TASTE WITHOUT SMELL

See how much you can taste without the help of your nose. Cut an apple, a carrot, some cheese, and other foods with a similar texture into cubes. Cover your eyes and nose and ask a friend to give you the pieces one by one. Can you taste the difference? Try the test on your friend too.

Most people can identify about 3,000 different smells.

▽ **This photo** of taste buds was taken through a microscope. Our tongue has about 10,000 taste buds, which pick up the four basic tastes and pass the information on.

NEW WORDS

mucus A moist, sticky substance in the nose.

olfactory nerve A nerve that runs from the nose to the brain, taking messages about smells.

particle A very very small piece of something.

taste bud A sense organ on the tongue that helps us taste things.

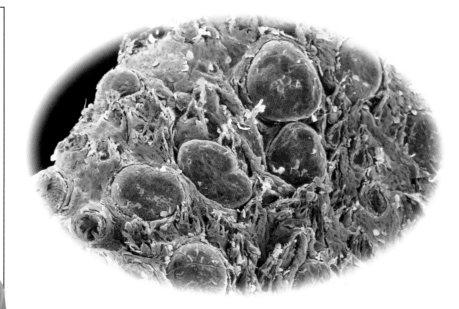

Babies have taste buds all over the inside of their mouths. They are also very sensitive to smells. As we grow older, our sense of smell gets weaker.

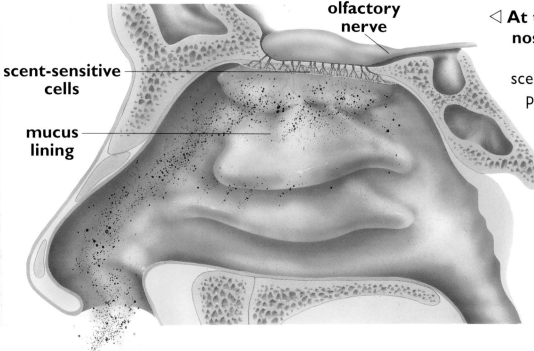

olfactory nerve

scent-sensitive cells

mucus lining

◁ **At the top of the nose** are cells that are sensitive to scent particles. The particles dissolve in a lining of mucus, and signals are sent along the olfactory nerve. This nerve leads to a special part of the brain, where smells are identified.

Hearing

hammer

anvil

stirrup

When we look at someone's ears, we see only a part of them. This part, called the outer ear, is shaped to collect sounds as they travel through the air.

All sounds are made by things vibrating. Sound waves make the eardrums and other parts vibrate. Information on vibrations is then sent to the brain, which lets us hear the sounds.

anvil

stirrup

hammer

△ **A tiny bone** called the hammer is connected to the eardrum. The eardrum vibrates the hammer. The hammer then moves the anvil, which in turn moves the stirrup bone. Finally, the stirrup vibrates the cochlea.

outer ear

eardrum

cochlea

△ **Sounds** pass into the ear and make the eardrum vibrate, which in turn vibrates tiny bones. The bones shake a spiral tube shaped like a snail shell, called the cochlea. Inside the cochlea is a fluid, which moves tiny hairs that send signals to the brain. Then we hear the sounds.

EARDRUM DRUM
To make a pretend eardrum, cut a large piece from a plastic bag. Stretch it over the top of a big can and hold it in place with a rubber band. Sprinkle some sugar onto the plastic. Then hold a metal tray near to it and hit the tray with a wooden spoon. The grains of sugar will jump about as your drum vibrates with the sound.

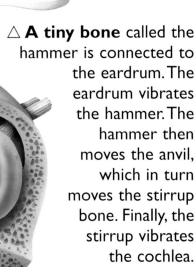

▽ **An old-fashioned ear trumpet** worked by acting as a bigger outer ear and making sounds louder. Modern hearing aids have tiny microphones and speakers.

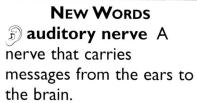

Have you ever felt your ears pop in a plane or an elevator? This sometimes happens when air pressure outside changes and is equalized in the middle ear.

▽ **Sounds travel well** through liquids, so it is easy to hear when you are underwater. Whales and other sea creatures make sounds to communicate with each other.

△ **Three canals** next to the cochlea, in the inner ear, help us keep our balance. They let the brain know what movements the body is making. Ballet dancers need excellent balance.

Seeing

We use our eyes to see. Rays of light come into each eye through an opening called the pupil, which is in the middle.

A lens inside each eye then bends the light very precisely, so that it travels to an area at the back of the eye called the retina.

The light rays make an image on the retina, but the image is upside down. Nerves send information on the image to the brain, which lets us see it the right way up.

▽ **Our eyes** are about the size of table-tennis balls, but we only see a small part at the front when we look in the mirror. The pupil is surrounded by a colored iris, which has a clear protective shield in front of it, called the cornea.

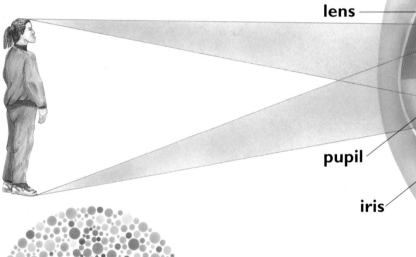

cornea ————

lens ————

pupil

iris

△ **Most people see** things in color, but some are color blind. This is a test card for color blindness. Can you see the shape inside the circle?

▷ **The color** of our eyes is really just the color of the iris. We inherit this color from our parents, and the most common color is brown. If one parent has blue eyes and the other brown, their child will usually have brown eyes.

▷ **Many people** wear glasses or contact lenses to help them see better. These change the direction of light before it enters the eyes, so that it focuses better on the retina.

optic nerve

day

night

retina

NEW WORDS

cornea The clear protective layer that covers the pupil.

iris The colored part of the eye surrounding the pupil.

pupil The opening at the front of the eye that lets in light.

retina The layer at the back of the eye that is sensitive to light.

You blink about 15 times each minute, without thinking about it. The brain controls many actions such as this automatically.

△ **When it is sunny or a bright day,** our eyes do not need to let in much light, and our pupils are small. But when there is less light, like at nighttime, the pupils have to open more and they get bigger. Small muscles change the size of the iris around the pupil.

About one in every 12 men find it very difficult to tell the difference between some colors, especially red and green. Very few women are color blind.

119

▷ **Blind people** can read and write using a system called Braille. The letters of the Braille alphabet are a system of raised dots, which can be felt and understood through the fingertips.

The Braille alphabet was invented by a Frenchman named Louis Braille (1809-1852). He went blind at the age of three, and later became an organ player and a professor.

▷ **Every person's fingertips** have a different skin pattern, called a fingerprint. These are the main fingerprint patterns.

arch　　　　loop　　　　whorl

NEW WORDS

fingerprint The pattern made by the tips of the fingers.

Braille A system of reading and writing for the blind.

axon The long, threadlike part of a nerve cell.

Our hands and the soles of our feet have many nerve endings. They have skin up to 1/8 inch (3 mm) thick, which is much thicker than on other parts of the body.

▽ **Nerve endings** lie just beneath the surface of the skin. They send messages along threadlike axons.

Nerve signals can travel through the body at 240 mph (400 kph), so they reach the brain very quickly!

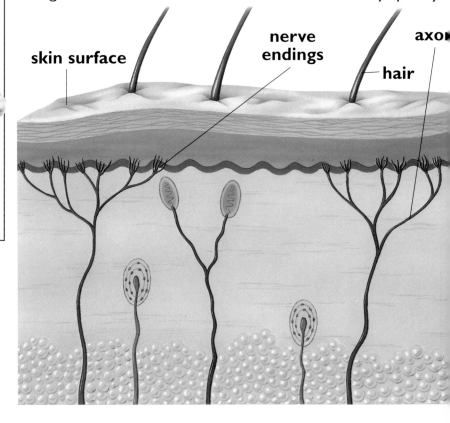

skin surface

nerve endings

axon

hair

Touching

When we touch things, nerve endings just under the surface of the skin send messages to the brain through the central nervous system. The brain interprets the messages, and we feel things.

Our nerves can help us feel hardness, softness and sharpness, for example. We can also feel heat and cold. Some parts of the body, such as our fingertips, have many more nerve endings than others.

▽ **Our sense of touch** gives us information about the world. It allows us to learn about things around us without seeing them.

TOUCHY-FEELY GAME
Put lots of separate objects in a bag. Choose things that feel different, such as an apple, an orange, a soft toy, a brush, a stone, a pencil, and so on. Ask a friend to put one hand in the bag and guess what they can feel. Then ask your friend to put different things in the bag for you to have your turn.

How Babies Grow

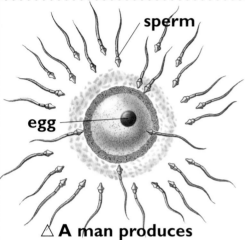

△ A man produces sperm. When one sperm joins up with a woman's egg, the fertilized egg starts to grow and develop into a baby.

Each of us began life as a tiny cell inside our mother's body. One of our father's cells joined up with one of our mother's egg cells. The egg cell then grew, to make a baby.

Babies grow in the part of a woman's body called the womb. It takes about nine months for the cell to grow into a fully formed baby. As the baby gets bigger, the mother's womb stretches to make room for it. When it is ready, the mother's muscles start to push the baby out of her body and into the world.

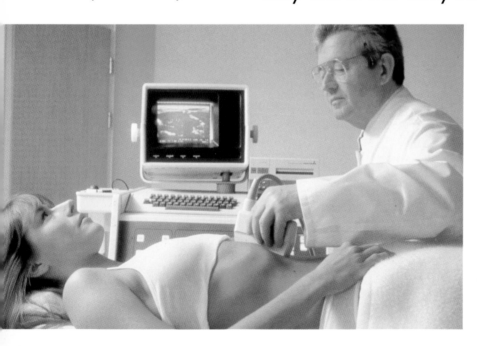

◁ **Doctors** can check on a baby's health before it is born. They use a special scanner that shows a picture of the inside of the mother's womb. They can even see whether the baby is a boy or a girl.

A baby is about 20 inches (50 cm) long at birth. When she gives birth, the mother is usually helped by a special doctor, called an obstetrician.

▷ **These are the organs** which help a woman and a man make a baby. Eggs are made in a woman's ovaries. They then move down the fallopian tubes next to the womb. Sperm is made in a man's testicles, and moves through tubes to the penis.

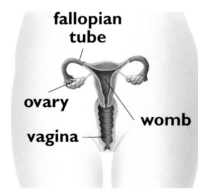

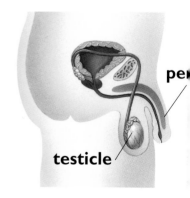

▷ **When children are born** to the same parents, they are brothers or sisters. Sometimes a mother has two babies at the same time, and these are called twins. They share the same birthday throughout their lives.

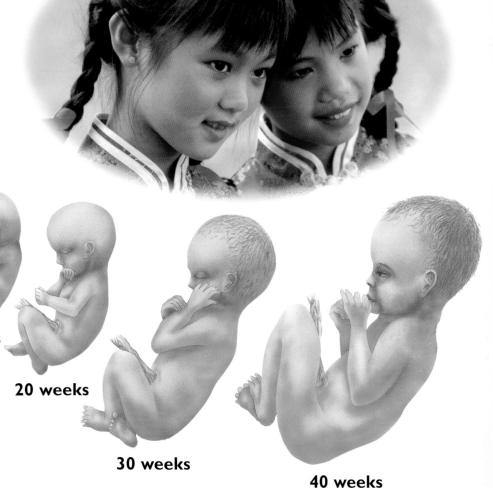

...eks

8 weeks

12 weeks

20 weeks

30 weeks

40 weeks

△ **A baby grows** very quickly in a bag of warm liquid in the womb. After eight weeks, it is about 1 3/4 inches (4 cm) long and has all its important body organs.

NEW WORDS

ovary An organ in a woman's body where egg cells are produced.

sperm A male cell that joins with a female egg to make a baby.

umbilical cord The tube that feeds a baby food and oxygen from its mother's body when it is in the womb.

womb The organ in a woman's body where a baby grows.

Inside the womb a baby floats in a watery fluid. It gets food and oxygen from its mother's body, through a tube called the umbilical cord.

▽ **The mother** may give birth in a hospital, or at home. When the baby's umbilical cord is cut, it leaves a mark called the navel, or belly button.

Growing Up

Babies need a lot of love and care, because they cannot look after themselves. But babies grow and learn very quickly, so that, as young children, they can soon do a lot of things for themselves.

By the time a child is two years old, it is about half the height it will be as an adult. Young children go on growing quickly, reaching three quarters of their adult height by the age of about nine.

Children go on to become teenagers and then young adults. As adults they may leave their parents and eventually have children of their own.

△ **A baby** learns a huge amount in a short space of time. She learns to use her hands and feet to crawl and push herself up, before standing up and taking her first proper steps.

NEW WORDS

college A place where you can go after school to continue with your learning.

retire To stop working—usually when you are old.

△ **Children** love playing, and they learn a lot through play. When children play together, they learn about helping each other as well as about the objects and materials they play with.

As people grow older, their bodies' cells cannot replace themselves so quickly. This means it takes longer for damaged parts of the body to get better.

How tall?
The world's tallest person was Robert Wadlow (1918-1940). He was taller than most adults by the age of ten, and finally reached a height of 8 feet, 11 inches (2.72 m). That is over half as tall again as many grown-up people.

◁ **Children playing at the beach** have a lot of fun. At the same time (and without realizing it), they learn a great deal about themselves and the world around them.

The oldest person in the world was Jeanne Calment, who was born in France in 1875. She died in 1997, at the age of 122 years.

▽ **Old people** usually retire from their jobs, as their bodies start to slow down. Then they may be able to spend time doing things they enjoy, such as woodworking or gardening.

Teenagers are young adults. When they finish school, they may go on to a college. They start to make their own decisions and become independent.

△ **Most children** enjoy going to school where they make friends with other children and have fun. They also learn about many interesting things and play lots of games.

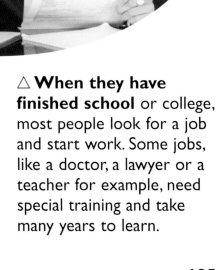

△ **When they have finished school** or college, most people look for a job and start work. Some jobs, like a doctor, a lawyer or a teacher for example, need special training and take many years to learn.

Keeping Healthy

To stay healthy, we have to look aft[er] our bodies. We can make sure that we eat properly, get plenty of exercise, get as much sleep as we need, and keep ourselves clean.

Sometimes there is nothing you can do to stop yourself getting sick. But if you lead a healthy life, you will probably be able to get better much more quickly.

We can all avoid doing things that we know damage the body, such as smoking cigarettes, drinking too much alcohol, or taking harmful drugs.

△ **Exercise** helps keep our muscles, as well as the heart and lungs, working well. It also helps keep bones strong. But if you are not used to exercise, don't suddenly do too much.

◁ **Washing with soap and water** helps keep us clean and get rid of germs. You should always wash your hands after you have been to the toilet.

△ **Sometimes we need to go to the hospital,** where doctors and nurses help make us better again. If you were to break a bone, you would need to go to a hospital for treatment.

◁ **Flies and other animals** can spread germs and disease. That is why it is very important to store and serve food carefully, so that it stays fresh and is healthy for us to eat.

NEW WORDS

aerobics Exercises, usually to music, that keep you in shape and help to strengthen your muscles, heart and lungs.

alcohol A strong drink that can make you feel drunk, such as wine, beer, or liquor.

vaccinate To give someone a pill or injection to help protect them against an illness.

▽ **When we are ill,** the doctor may give us pills or medicine to help make us better. You must follow the doctor's instructions and never take pills without first asking for permission.

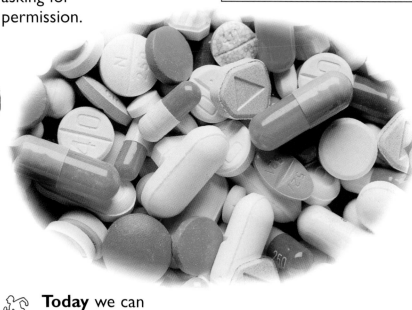

▽ **Many adults go to a gym** or a sports club to have a workout and keep fit. Dance exercises and aerobics are very popular.

Today we can be vaccinated against many diseases, either by injection or by mouth. Vaccination gives us a mild, harmless form of the disease and stops us getting it later.

Taking part in sport is an enjoyable way to get lots of exercise. Swimming helps to make you strong and supple, and jogging is good for stamina.

Doing dance exercises can help to make you more supple and will improve your stamina. For athletes, these sorts of exercises may be part of an overall fitness program.

Quiz

1. **Which part of the body** helps us to think and move? *(page 90)*

2. **We are made up of billions of tiny living units -** what are they called? *(page 91)*

3. **What is the name** of our framework of bones? *(page 92)*

4. **Are you likely to be shorter** or taller in the evening? *(page 93)*

5. **Roughly how many muscles** are there in the human body? *(page 94)*

6. **Which muscle** works together with the biceps? *(page 95)*

7. **Which blood vessels** carry blood away from the heart? *(page 96)*

8. **How many pints** of blood does an adult body contain? *(page 97)*

9. **Does your heart beat faster** or slower when you run? *(page 98)*

10. **What do asthma sufferers** use to help them breathe? *(page 99)*

11. **What vibrate** in your throat to make sounds? *(page 100)*

12. **Why do** we cough? *(page 101)*

13. **Which half of the brain** controls the left side of the body? *(page 102)*

14. **Where is** the spinal cord? *(page 103)*

15. **How much sleep** do babies need in a day? *(page 104)*

16. **What might you do** when your body needs extra oxygen? *(page 105)*

17. **Can different people** have the same fingerprints? *(page 106)*

18. **What are** our nails made of? *(page 107)*

19. **What are** our pointed teeth called? *(page 108)*

20. **What can you wear** to make crooked teeth straight? *(page 109)*

21. **Where does mixed-up food go** after it leaves the stomach? *(page 110)*

22. **What does** the large intestine do? *(page 111)*

23. **Why is fiber** useful to us? *(page 112)*

24. **What type of food** are bread and pasta? *(page 113)*

25. **Which part of the tongue** tastes bitter things? *(page 114)*

26. **Which nerve** runs from the nose to the brain? *(page 115)*

27. **Which bone** does the hammer move? *(page 116)*

28. **Can sound travel** through liquids? *(page 117)*

29. **What part of the eye** bends light? *(page 118)*

30. **In bright light,** are our pupils big or small? *(page 119)*

31. **What is the alphabet system** for blind people called? *(page 120)*

32. **Where do nerve endings** send messages? *(page 121)*

33. **In which part of a mother's body** does a baby grow? *(page 122)*

34. **What is another word** for belly button? *(page 123)*

35. **How tall** was the world's tallest person? *(page 124)*

36. **How old** is a teenager? *(page 125)*

37. **What can help keep our muscles,** heart and lungs working well? *(page 126)*

38. **What does** vaccination do? *(page 127)*

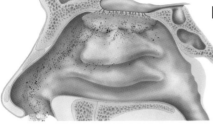
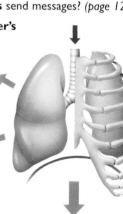
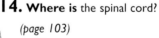
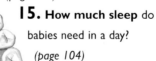

Animals

The wildlife kingdom is full of all sorts of amazing animals—mammals, reptiles, birds, amphibians, fish, insects, mollusks, and crustaceans. They live in all parts of the world, in different habitats and with different life cycles and behavior. There is a lot to learn about them, and there are things we can learn from them.

Which mammals can fly? What is a marsupial? Where do penguins live? These and hundreds more questions have fascinating answers, telling us more about the creatures with which we share our planet. We can also learn to respect and look after those animals that are threatened by the way humans live.

Mammals

There are many animals in the group we call mammals. Human beings are mammals, too. A mammal has hair or fur on its body, to help keep it warm. Baby mammals are fed with milk from their mother's body.

Mammals live all over the world, from the freezing polar regions to the hot tropics. Most mammals live on land, but whales live in the sea and bats can fly. They are known as warm-blooded animals.

△ **There are more than 400** different breeds of sheep. We shear them so that we can use their furry coats to make wool.

◁ **A porcupine** has long spines, called quills. It can raise and rattle its quills to warn off any of its enemies.

△ **Some mammals,** such as this otter, have whiskers. These help them feel things and find their way about.

◁ **Bears** are large mammals with powerful legs and strong claws. They eat plants as well as meat. They live mainly on the ground but can stand on their back legs and can even climb trees.

The largest mammal is the blue whale. The largest on land is the African elephant. The tallest is the giraffe. The fastest is the cheetah. And the smallest is the tiny hog-nosed bat.

▷ **The white rhinoceros** is one of the world's five species of rhino. They all have horns and for this reason are under threat from hunters.

△ **Kudu antelopes** have beautifully curved horns. Males sometimes use these to fight each other. Kudus live in small groups in Africa, and their main enemies are leopards, lions, and wild dogs.

NEW WORDS

✿ **breed** A variety of animal.

✿ **descendant** A person or animal that has come by birth from another person or animal.

✿ **tropics** The hottest part of the world, which is near the Equator.

△ **Farmyard pigs** are descendants of wild boars. Farmers keep them for their meat, which we call pork, ham and bacon. The female pig, called a sow, lies down to feed milk to all her piglets at the same time.

SNOWED IN

Female polar bears dig a den in a snowdrift in the freezing Arctic region. There they give birth to their cubs in midwinter, protecting them from the severe cold and wind. The tiny cubs stay in the den for about three months. Their mother feeds them with her own milk, though she eats nothing herself. Mother and cubs come out onto the snow and ice in spring. Mother then spends most of her time looking for food, such as seals.

131

Apes and Monkeys

Apes are generally larger than monkeys, and they have no tails. There are four types of ape. Gorillas and chimpanzees live only in Africa, and orangutans and gibbons live only in Southeast Asia.

Many different types of old world monkeys are found in both Africa and Asia. The new world monkeys of Central and South America have long tails, which they often use to hold on to branches as they swing through the trees. Most apes and monkeys live in the world's rain forests, many of which are being destroyed.

△ **Male mandrills** have very colorful faces. Mandrills live in African forests, staying mainly on the ground in troops of up to 50 animals. They feed on fruit, nuts, and small animals, and sleep in trees.

▷ **Many monkeys**, such as this macaque, live together in large troops. Each troop has a leader, usually an old, strong male. They spend most of their time in trees and have good eyesight, hearing, and sense of smell.

NEW WORDS
grooming Cleaning the skin and fur.
timber Wood that is used for building or making things.
troop An organized group.

▷ **Orangutans** live in the tropical rainforests of Borneo and Sumatra. In the Malay language, this ape's name means "man of the forest." In many places, its home is being cut down for timber. Reserves have been set up to protect it.

▽ **The gorilla** is the largest ape. Males are sometimes over 6 feet (1.8 m) tall, the same height as a tall man. They are powerful, but they are also peaceful and gentle. They rarely climb trees.

△ **Grooming** each other to get rid of irritating pests is an enjoyable group activity for these chimpanzees.

▷ **South American spider monkeys** have amazing tails which can wrap round and cling to branches.

 **Chimpanzees** are good tool-makers. They use sticks to get honey and insects from nests, and they use stones to crack nuts.

MONKEY MOBILE
Trace the monkey (right) and cut out its shape. Draw around the shape on cardboard and cut it out. Make two more monkeys and draw on faces. Make a small hole in each monkey and tie on pieces of thread. Tie the monkeys to some rolled cardboard. When the monkeys are balanced, fix the knots with a drop of glue.

Elephants

△ **Elephants** have thick, wrinkled skin. Their eyesight is not very good, but they have good hearing and an excellent sense of smell.

▷ **An elephant's tusks** are really two big teeth made of ivory. They are useful for digging and breaking off large branches. The trunk can be used to pick up food and guide it into an elephant's mouth.

▽ **Elephants love bathing.** They can give themselves a shower through their trunks and are good swimmers.

There are two species (or two different kinds), of elephant—African and Asian. The African elephant has large ears and is the world's biggest land animal. Males can grow up to 13 feet (4 m) high at the shoulder, which is over twice as tall as a man. They can weigh up to 7 tons, which is as much as 90 people! Asian elephants are smaller and lighter, with smaller ears. They live in India, Sri Lanka, and parts of Southeast Asia.

△ **A tree** is useful for scratching an annoying itch!

NEW WORDS

herd A large group of animals living together.

logging Cutting down trees to use the wood.

trunk An elephant's long, bendy nose.

tusk One of the two long pointed teeth sticking out of an elephant's mouth.

▷ **Asian elephants** are used in the logging industry, because they can move and carry very heavy loads. Riders sit behind the animal's neck. In some countries, elephants are still used as a means of getting around.

 **Elephants sometimes use** their trunks as snorkels. When they swim, they can stick their trunks upward so that they breathe in plenty of air.

Do elephants use skin care?
Yes! To prevent their skin from cracking, elephants wallow and cover themselves in cool mud. This dries on their bodies and helps protect them from the burning sun. It also gets rid of flies and ticks. An elephant's color depends on the mud it wallows in.

◁ **Elephants** can reach food high up in trees. They are vegetarians, and their diet includes leaves, fruit, bark, and roots.

Elephants live in family groups, which often join together to make large herds. Each group is led by a female elephant, who is usually the oldest. She decides which routes the herd should follow to find food and water, often traveling in single file.

Cats

There are a number of species, or different kinds, of cats. Even the biggest wild cats are relatives of our pet cats at home!

Pet cats are used to living with people, and to being fed by their owners. But sometimes they hunt, chasing after birds and mice before pouncing. While lions and tigers roar, a pet cat just meows!

All cats are carnivores. They are built to hunt, and their bodies are powerful. To help them catch their prey, cats have sharp eyesight and a good sense of smell. They can run very fast too. Their size, coloring, and coat patterns vary, but all cats have a similar shape.

△ **Cheetahs** are the fastest cats. In fact, they are the fastest runners in the world. They can reach a speed of 60 mph (100 kph) for a short distance.

Tigers are the biggest cats. From head to tail they are up to 12 feet (3.6 m) long. These powerful animals make very good mothers to their baby cubs.

puma

jaguar

▷ **Members of the cat family:** they look alike but live in different ways.

▷ **Male and female lions** look very different. The male has a big brown mane. Lions are the only cats that live together in groups, called prides. Lions like to sit around and let the lionesses do most of the hunting.

◁ **The top male** lion is challenged by other males in the pride from time to time. He has to fight them in order to keep his position as the dominant male in the group.

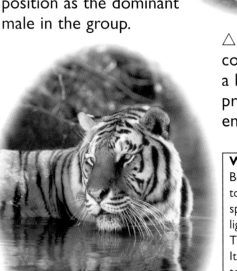

△ **Big cats** like flat, open country, where they can see a long way. They follow their prey until they are close enough to strike.

▷ **Pet cats** and many of the big cats don't like water. But tigers search it out during the hottest part of the day. Then they are often found cooling off in a pool. They are excellent swimmers and can easily cross rivers.

Why do leopards have spots?
Because they make leopards difficult to see. From a distance, the black spots on the yellow fur look like light on the grass or in the trees. This is called camouflage. It helps the leopard to hide from the animals it is hunting, and from those hunting it.

leopard

black anther

lynx

cheetah

lions

NEW WORDS
🐾**carnivore** An animal that eats meat.
🐾**coat** The fur on an animal.
🐾**mane** Long, thick hair growing around a male lion's neck. Horses have manes too.
🐾**prey** An animal hunted by another for food.
🐾**pride** A group of lions, lionesses and cubs that live together.
🐾**dominant** To be the most important animal, or the leader, among a group of animals.

WHALES TO SCALE

Draw whales and dolphins in scale with each other. You can use the scale 1:144. This means using an inch for every 12 feet, so your blue whale will be 9 inches long. The whales' real lengths are: common dolphin 6 feet, bottlenose dolphin 12 feet, narwhal 20 feet, pilot whale 25 feet, killer whale 30 feet, and the blue whale 108 feet.

△ **Pilot whales**, like the one at the top of the photo, have a big, round head. They live in large groups, called schools, of hundreds or even thousands. The other dolphin is a bottlenose.

NEW WORDS

baleen The whalebone at the front of some whales' mouths.

blowhole The nostril on top of a whale's head, through which it breathes.

dolphinarium A pool for dolphins, where they give public displays.

school A group of fish, whales, or dolphins.

▽ **The blue whale** is the largest animal in the world. It can grow up to 108 feet (33 m) long and weigh over 150 tons. Blue whales swim in all the world's oceans, usually alone or in small groups.

△ **These common dolphins** are leaping out of the water at great speed. Most dolphins swim at about 20 mph (30 kph). This is over three times faster than even the quickest human swimmers can manage.

Instead of teeth, blue whales have strips of whalebone, called baleen. When the whales take in water, the baleen traps tiny shrimps called krill.

Other whales, such as killer whales and sperm whales, have teeth. Dolphins are small-toothed whales.

Whales and Dolphins

△ **The narwhal** is a small Arctic whale with a long tusk.

Whales and dolphins are mammals, **and they cannot breathe underwater like fish. So they come to the surface often, to take in air.** Whales and dolphins breathe in and out through a blowhole on the top of the head. When they let out used air, they usually send out a spray of water at the same time.

△ **Some whales and dolphins** are kept in zoos and dolphinariums. Killer whales are very popular performers. They can jump as high as 16 feet (5 m).

▷ **Many whales and dolphins** live and hunt for their food in groups. They eat fish, squid, and shrimps.

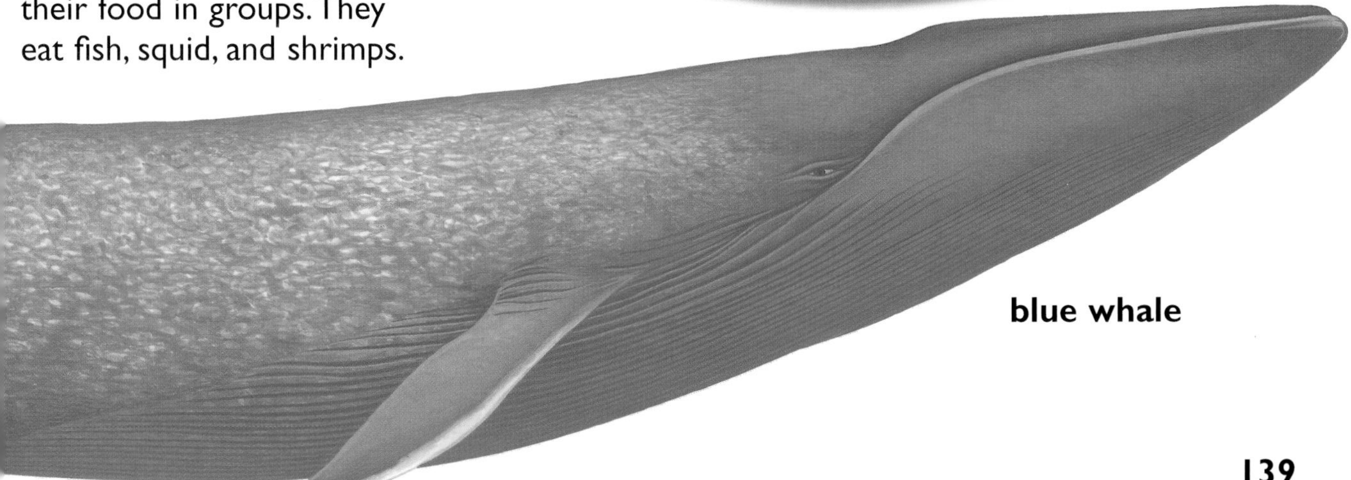

blue whale

139

Bats

Bats are different from all other mammals in one way: they can fly. They do not have feathery wings like birds but, instead, have double layers of skin stretched over thin bones.

There are nearly a thousand different kinds of bats. Most are nocturnal, which means that they are active only at night. They sleep during the day and come out at night to find food. Most bats live on insects alone, but some eat fruit and nectar and others even hunt small animals. Bats live in almost every part of the world, except in the cold polar regions.

△ **All bats** have large, sensitive ears to steer by. These help them pick up echoes of the high-pitched sounds they make. Most bats have razor-sharp teeth.

Bats are relatively small creatures with large wings. A vampire bat's body is only about 4 inches (10 cm) long, but it has a wingspan of up to 7 inches (18 cm).

▽ **A bat's long arm** ends in four fingers and a strong, hook-shaped thumb. When its wings are folded, the bat can use its thumbs to climb trees or rocks.

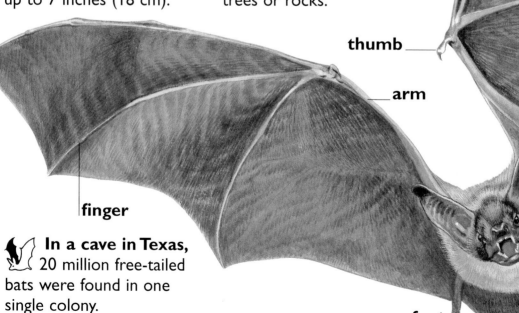

thumb___

___arm

finger

In a cave in Texas, 20 million free-tailed bats were found in one single colony.

foot

tail

▷ **Bats hang upside down** by their feet when they rest or sleep. They often live in caves, where there may be thousands of bats crowded together on the walls and ceiling. Smaller bat colonies of up to 12 bats may live together inside a hollow tree.

△ **Bats use echoes** from their high-pitched squeaks to catch insects. The echoes help the bats make up a sound picture of what is around them. They do not need to use their eyes so much, but it is not true that they are "as blind as a bat."

Do bats fish?
Some bats really do fish, in the same way that some birds do. The fisherman (or bulldog) bat of Mexico lives near mangrove swamps. When it hunts, it swoops down near the water. Then the bat dips quickly into the water with its clawlike feet, catches a small fish and scoops it up into its mouth.

▽ **Three different bat faces.** The vampire bat lives in Central and South America. It uses its sharp teeth and tubelike tongue to suck animals' blood.

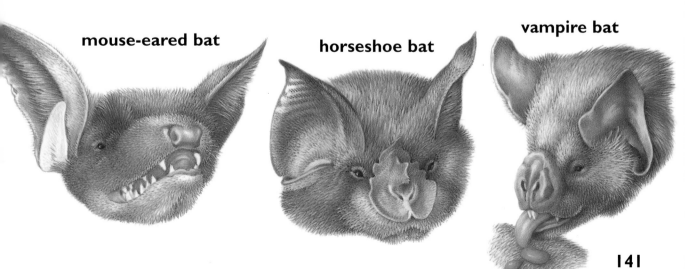

mouse-eared bat

horseshoe bat

vampire bat

141

Marsupials

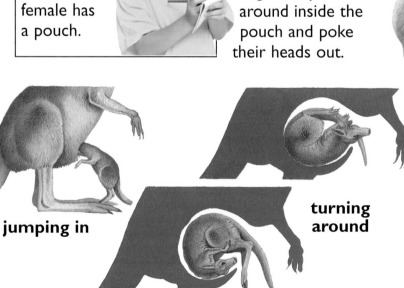

Marsupials are a special group of mammals. Unlike all other animals, female marsupials have a pouch. They give birth to tiny babies, who stay in the pouch and live off their mother's milk until they are big enough to venture into the outside world. The soft pouch is warm and snug.

Most marsupials, like kangaroos, koalas, and wombats, live in Australia. Some smaller kinds, called opossums, live in North and South America.

△ **Wallabies** are like small kangaroos. This unusual wallaby is called an albino—it has white fur and pink eyes. Most wallabies are gray or brown.

NEW WORDS
**albino** An animal that has very little color in its skin, hair, and eyes.
joey A baby kangaroo.
marsupial A type of mammal in which the female has a pouch.

▽ **Baby kangaroos** are called joeys. When they are old enough to leave the pouch, they jump back in if there is danger. They turn around inside the pouch and poke their heads out.

jumping in

turning around

▽ **The tiny honey possum** feeds on pollen and nectar. Its 4 inch (10 cm) tail, which it uses for gripping like some monkeys, is longer than its body.

◁ **A female kangaroo** and her joey. Joeys have an easy time, sitting in the pouch while their mother finds food. Kangaroos hop on their huge back legs and can travel more than 30 feet (9 m) in one giant leap.

△ **Koalas** are expert climbers. They spend most of their time near the top of eucalyptus trees, eating the tender shoots. Although they look like small bears, koalas have nothing to do with the bear family.

ROO RACERS
Draw two kangaroos on cardboard and cut them out. Make a hole just below the head and run some string through. Tie one end of each length of string to a chair leg and lie the racers on their backs a couple of yards away. Then you and a friend can race your kangaroos by pulling on the string and then letting it go. The chair is the finishing line.

Reptiles

Snakes, lizards, and crocodiles are all reptiles. Unlike mammals, these scaly skinned animals are all cold-blooded. This means that they always need lots of sunshine to warm them up.

△ **Marine iguanas** are the only lizards that swim in the sea. They live around the Galapagos Islands, in the Pacific Ocean. They go to sea to feed on seaweed and then warm up on the islands' volcanic rocks.

The largest lizard is the Komodo dragon of Indonesia. It can grow up to 10 feet (3 m) long.

▽ **The horned lizard** has strong armour, to protect it from its enemies. It has pointed scales, as well as horns behind its head. It lives in dry areas and deserts of America, where it feeds mainly on ants. The female horned lizard lays her eggs in a hole in the ground.

A skink is a kind of lizard. It can make its tail fall off if when it is attacked by an enemy. This usually confuses the enemy, so that the lizard can quickly escape. It then grows a new tail.

Reptiles are found on land and in water. Most live in warm parts of the world, and some live in hot deserts. They move into a burrow if it is too hot above ground, or if it is ever too cold in winter.

Most reptiles have four legs, but snakes are long, legless reptiles. All snakes are meat-eaters, and some kill their prey with poison from hollow teeth called fangs.

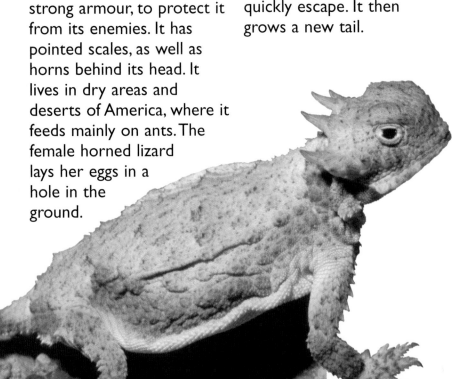

NEW WORDS
chameleon A lizard with a long tongue and the ability to change color.
fang A snake's long, pointed, hollow tooth, through which it can pass its poison.
marine Living in, or from, the sea.

▷ **Chameleons** are slow-moving, tree-living lizards. If they see an insect within range, they shoot out a long sticky tongue to catch it. They can also change color to suit their surroundings or their mood. An angry chameleon may turn black.

△ **Most reptiles lay eggs**, which are soft and leathery. Snakes lay their eggs in shallow holes and cover them with a thin layer of soil. When the baby snakes hatch out, they have to look after themselves.

The longest snake is the reticulated python of Southeast Asia, which grows up to 30 feet (9 m) long. The most poisonous snake is the small-scaled snake living in Australia.

▽ **Emerald tree boas** live in the rain forests of South America. They wrap themselves around branches and watch out for prey, often birds and bats. They move fast and also swim very well.

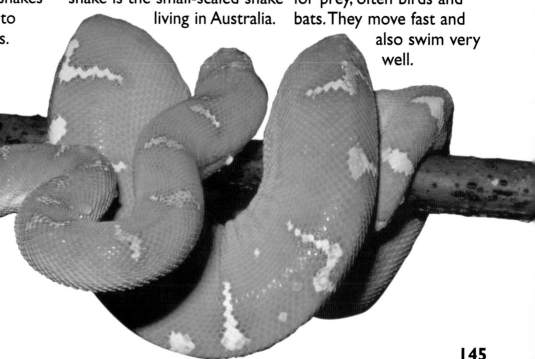

145

Crocodiles and Turtles

Crocodiles and alligators belong to a group of reptiles called crocodilians. They are large, powerful animals with long tails and strong jaws. Crocodilians live in or close to water and are found mainly in rivers in hot countries.

Turtles and tortoises have a hard shell made of bony plates. Turtles move slowly on land but are very good, fast swimmers. Tortoises however, spend all their time on land.

△ **American alligators** live in rivers and swamps of southeastern USA. They can grow more than 15 feet (4.5 m) long and eat fish, small mammals and birds.

During a long period of hot, dry weather, crocodiles may bury themselves deep in the mud and go to sleep. They will stay there until the weather changes.

▽ **The hawksbill turtle** is found near the rocky coasts and coral reefs of our oceans. The females lay about 150 eggs at a time.

▽ **Green turtles** spend most of their time at sea, only coming on land to sleep and to lay eggs. At nesting time they travel hundreds or even thousands of miles to lay eggs on the beach where they were born.

◁ **The gavial** is a type of crocodilian with a long, thin snout. It has about 100 sharp teeth, which it uses to catch fish and frogs. Gavials can be found in the big rivers of Malaysia. and northern India.

MAKE A JUNK CROC

Crunch sheets of newspaper up into different-sized balls and arrange them into a crocodile shape. Make two jaws and four legs, and then tape everything together. Mix some wallpaper paste and stick thin strips of newspaper all over the crocodile with the paste. Stick on three layers, and then leave it to dry. Add some jagged cardboard teeth, two eyes, and paint the croc green all over.

▷ **Female American alligators** and African crocodiles are caring mothers. When their babies have hatched, they carry them to a nearby pool in their mouths.

▽ **Giant tortoises** on the Galapagos Islands grow up to 54 inches (135 cm) long.

NEW WORDS

crocodilian Any one of a group of large reptiles that includes crocodiles and alligators.

reef A row of underwater rocks.

tortoise A large, slow-moving land turtle.

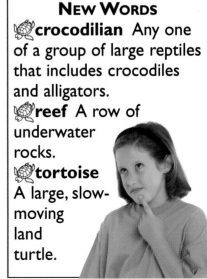

Birds

Birds are the only animals with feathers. They have wings, and most are expert fliers. There are more than 9,000 different kinds, living in all parts of the world.

Female birds lay eggs, and most build nests to protect them. When the eggs hatch out, the adults feed their young until the small birds can fly and leave the nest.

◁ **The Indian peacock** spreads his tail feathers into a fan. He does this to attract the female peahen.

▽ **Birds** have various beaks. With its beak, a macaw can crack nuts, a pelican scoops fish, and an eagle can tear meat.

△ **Gulls** and other seabirds spend much of their time at sea. They glide over the water, waiting to swoop down to catch fish. Many seabirds nest on rocky cliffs.

▽ **Arctic terns** raise their young near the North Pole. Then they fly south to the Antarctic for the summer. In the autumn they fly north again, making a round trip of 21,000 miles (36,000 km).

macaw

pelican

flamingo

DIFFERENT NESTS

osprey

horned grebe

barn swallow

weaver bird

willow flycatcher

ovenbird

bird of
paradise

BIRD OF PARADISE

Draw a bird of paradise on blue
cardboard with white crayon.
Cut out pieces of colored
paper to fit the head and body,
and stick feather shapes on the
body. Add long strips of tissue
paper for the tail, and don't
forget feet, a beak and a button
eye. You could make a rain
forest background too, with
real twigs and leaves.

toucan

bald eagle

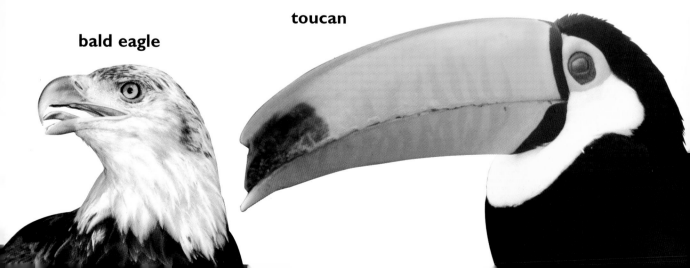

Birds of Prey

△ **The bald eagle** gets its name from its white head feathers. Bald eagles feed on fish, waterbirds, and rabbits. They live along coasts, rivers, and lakes in North America.

Birds that hunt animals for food are called birds of prey. Eagles, hawks, and falcons all have hooked beaks and strong, sharp talons.

They are fast fliers and have excellent long-distance eyesight. They can swoop down on their prey from a great height.

Most owls hunt at night and they can fly with hardly a sound. Their feathers have a soft fringe, to muffle the sound of their wings.

Vultures are scavengers. Other animals make a kill for them and then they eat the leftovers.

▷ **The osprey**, or fish-hawk, is found in most parts of the world. It is an excellent catcher of fish. The osprey circles over the water and then plunges in, feet forward, to snatch the fish in its talons. Sometimes the osprey dives right under the water to get the fish.

NEW WORDS
marrow The soft substance inside bones.
scavenger An animal that looks for and lives off scraps of dead meat killed by others.
talon A strong claw.

◁ **White-backed vultures** find plenty of food on the African grasslands. They wait for the big cats to have their meal first. After their own meal, vultures clean their feathers well, so that they are always in good flying condition.

PEREGRINE FALCON

talons

The peregrine falcon is the world's fastest bird. It can travel over 200 mph (350 kph) as it dives towards its prey. It eats other birds, especially pigeons.

Which birds use tools?
Egyptian vultures use stones as tools. They like to eat ostrich eggs, which are too big and tough to crack open with their beak. So the vultures pick up stones and drop them on the eggs to crack them. Then they feed on the insides.

△ **The lammergeier,** or bearded vulture, picks up bones and drops them onto rocks, to get at the marrow inside.

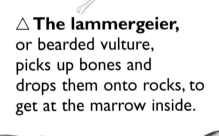

The condor of the Andes mountains in South America is the world's biggest bird of prey. Weighing up to 30 pounds, it can soar for long distances on its enormous wings. The condor has a wingspan of 10 feet (3 m) and flies at a height of up to 23,000 feet (7,000 m).

△ **Owls** have many advantages as night hunters. Their round face helps funnel sounds to their ear openings, which lie under feathered flaps. They can also turn their head right around, to see behind them with their large eyes.

△ **Rockhopper penguins** have long yellow or orange feathers above their eyes. They often nest on clifftops, using pebbles or grass. They reach their colony by hopping from rock to rock, as their name suggests.

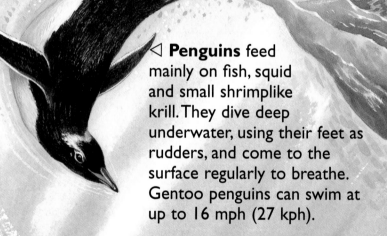

△ **After a winter at sea,** Snares Island penguins arrive at the islands of the same name, south of New Zealand. They return to these islands every August to breed again.

▽ **These Adélie penguins** are waddling about on an iceberg, off the coast of Antarctica. To climb out of the sea, penguins first dive down and then shoot out of the water at great speed, landing on their feet. To get back into the sea, they simply jump in.

◁ **Penguins** feed mainly on fish, squid and small shrimplike krill. They dive deep underwater, using their feet as rudders, and come to the surface regularly to breathe. Gentoo penguins can swim at up to 16 mph (27 kph).

Penguins

Like all the world's birds, penguins are covered with feathers. But penguin feathers are short and thick. They are waterproof, and keep the animals warm in cold seas.

Penguins have a horny beak for catching food. They also have a small pair of wings, but nevertheless, can't fly. They use their wings as flippers. These birds spend most of their time at sea and are fast, skilful swimmers.

There are 18 different kinds of penguin, and they all live near the coasts of the cold southern oceans. Many live in the frozen region of Antarctica.

emperor penguin

little blue penguin

▷ **The smallest penguins** are "little blues" standing 16 inches (40 cm) high. Emperor penguins are the biggest at 48 inches (120 cm) tall.

△ **Antarctic emperor penguins** keep their eggs and chicks on their feet, for warmth. It is the male bird who does this job, while the female feeds her young.

NEW WORDS
chick A baby bird, such as a young penguin.
krill Tiny shrimplike creatures that are eaten by penguins and whales.

A PENGUIN PLAYMATE
Pour sand into an empty plastic bottle and tape a washball to the top. Tape a cardboard beak to the head. Mix wallpaper paste and paste thin strips of newspaper over the penguin. When it's dry, paint the penguin white. Leave to dry again before painting the head, back and flippers black, leaving white circles for the eyes. You could use your penguin as a bookend.

Amphibians

Frogs, toads, newts, and salamanders belong to a group of animals called amphibians. They spend part of their lives on land and part in water, but amphibians don't live in the sea.

Amphibians go back to water when it is time to lay their eggs. Females may lay their eggs in or near a pond or stream. Most frogs and toads lay between 1,000 and 20,000 eggs. These large clusters of eggs are called spawn.

△ **Tree frogs** have round suckers at the end of their toes. These help them to grip trunks, branches, and even shiny leaves.

▷ **Large North American bullfrogs** can grow up to 8 inches (20 cm) long. This bullfrog has caught an earthworm, but they eat much larger prey too. A big bullfrog might catch a mouse or even a small snake.

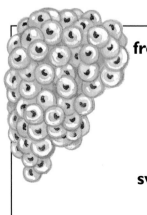

frogs eggs or spawn

froglet with legs

swimming tadpole

FROG LIFE CYCLE
A frog's eggs hatch into tadpoles in the water. The tadpoles grow legs and turn into froglets. Finally the young frogs can leave the water and hop out onto land.

young frog

◁ **This smooth-skinned giant salamander** lives in the rivers, lakes, and cool, damp forests of western USA. It can grow to 12 inches (30 cm) long. Most salamanders are silent, but this one can make a low-pitched cry.

What are mouth-brooders?
A male mouth-brooding frog can gather up to 15 eggs with its tongue and put them in its mouth. But it doesn't eat the eggs. It keeps them in its vocal sac to turn into tadpoles. When the froglets are ready, they jump out.

▷ **Arrow-poison frogs** of South America are very poisonous. Females lay up to six eggs on land. When they hatch, the male carries the tadpoles on his back to a tree hole filled with water or to a water plant, so that they can begin life in water.

Toads usually have a rougher, bumpier skin than frogs which is often covered with warts. Toads usually live in drier places. They have wider bodies and shorter, less powerful legs, which means that they are not such good jumpers.

NEW WORDS

froglet A young frog that develops from a tadpole.

spawn The mass of eggs produced by amphibians.

tadpole The young frog or toad that develops from an egg and lives in water.

vocal sac Loose folds of skin in male frogs that can fill with air to make a noise.

△ **Frogs** have long back legs. These are good for swimming and we copy their action when we swim breaststroke. These powerful legs are also useful for jumping on land. Common frogs can leap about 2 feet (60 cm), and South African sharp-nosed frogs can jump over 10 feet (3 m)!

Female surinam toads keep their eggs in holes in their skin. The young toads develop in these holes.

Fish

There are more than 20,000 different kinds of fish in the world's oceans, lakes, and rivers. Like other animals, fish live in warm parts of the world, as well as in cold polar seas.

Many fish have streamlined bodies and fins, to help them swim. They have gills instead of lungs, so that they can breathe under water.

Fish have the same body temperature as the waters in which they live and swim.

◁ **The butterfly fish** has beautiful colors and strong contrasting markings.

▽ **The lionfish** has fins sticking out all over its body, and a row of poisonous spines. It grows up to 15 inches (38 cm) long.

△ **Some fish** have amazing defences. This porcupine fish has swollen up into a spiny ball. It must have sensed danger nearby.

▽ **Salmon** have to work very hard to make their way upriver from the ocean to breed. They swim against the current of the river and leap over the shallow, rocky parts.

NEW WORDS

breed To produce babies.

fin A thin flat part that sticks out of a fish's body and helps it to swim.

gill The parts of their bodies through which fishes breathe.

streamlined Shaped smoothly for moving faster.

156

▽ **The ray** has a flat body, which helps it glide along the bottom of the sea. Rays feed mainly on shellfish, which they crack open with their strong teeth. Some kinds of rays can sting with their tails.

SEE THE SEA WORLD
Cut one side of a box to make a window. Use crumpled-up tissue paper to make the seabed. Cut out waves. Make lots of fish out of colored paper and stick thread to them. Tape all the threads to the top of your own sea world.

HOW FISH BREATHE

1. A fish takes in water through its mouth.

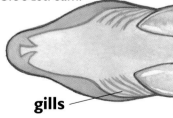

2. The water flows over its gills and oxygen passes into its bloodstream.

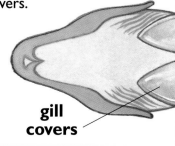

gills

3. The water is then pushed back out through the gill covers.

gill covers

▷ **Seahorses** look very strange. They swim in an upright position and live near seaweed, which they can hold on to with their tails. Seahorses are a fish which can change color.

▷ **This trumpet fish** is long and thin, growing up to 3 feet (0.9 m) long. Its eyes are set well back from its jaws. Compare its shape to the ray and the porcupine fish.

▽ **Moray eels** usually swim along with their mouths open, ready to catch smaller fish.

Electric eels kill fish and other sea animals with electric shocks from their tail. These big South American fish are up to 6 feet (1.8 m) long.

Sharks

Sharks are the fierce hunters of the world's oceans. People are very frightened of them, though many sharks are quite harmless.

Most fish have an air bag, called a swim bladder, which helps to keep them afloat. Sharks don't have a swim bladder, which means they have to keep swimming all the time, or else they would sink to the bottom. Sharks are different from most other fish in another way too. A shark's skeleton is made of rubbery cartilage instead of bone.

△ **Some sharks lay eggs** rather than giving birth to live babies. They lay their eggs in a tough case, which we call a mermaid's purse. The baby fish grow inside the case, which attaches itself to weeds.

△ **The great white shark** is the most famous of all the sharks. It grows up to 20 feet (6 m) long, or more.

🦈**cartilage** Tough rubbery gristle, which is more bendy than bone and makes up the skeleton of sharks, rays, and skates.

🦈**mermaid's purse** A tough case containing shark's eggs.

🦈**swim bladder** An air-filled bag inside a fish's body that helps keep it afloat.

△ **Shark's teeth** form double or triple rows and are set inside a tooth bed. New teeth are formed in grooves in this area every 1-2 weeks to replace old or worn-out teeth.

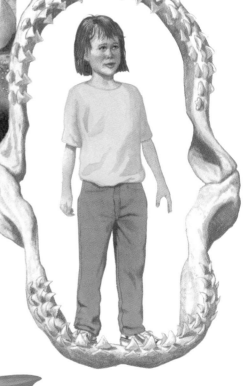

nurse shark

🦈**The whale shark** is the world's largest fish, growing over 40 feet (12 m) long. But this shark is not dangerous. It uses its huge mouth as a scoop for catching and eating tiny sea creatures. The smallest shark is the dwarf shark at just 6 inches (15 cm) long.

tiger shark

△ **Tiger sharks** are thought to be dangerous to people, but any shark will only attack if it smells blood. All sharks have an excellent sense of smell and good hearing, helping them hunt at night.

▷ **Reef sharks** live near coral reefs, where there are plenty of smaller fish and other sea creatures for them to feed on.

Insects

head

antennae

thorax

abdomen

△ **This wasp** shows the three basic body parts of an insect—a head, a thorax, and an abdomen. Its legs and wings are attached to the thorax, and its antennae to the head.

▽ **This honey bee** is collecting nectar and pollen from a flower. The bee will take the food to its nest, where it will be stored as honey.

Insects are tiny animals that are found all over the world—from scorching deserts to steaming rain forests and icy lakes.

Insects have no backbone, and they are protected by a hard, outer skeleton or shell. Because they are so small, they can fit into tiny places and don't need much food to live on. They all have six legs, and most have wings and can fly. Many insects have two pairs of wings, but flies have just one pair.

termite mound

food store

queen's chamber

tunnel

egg chamber

▷ **Termites** live in colonies and build huge mounds as nests. Each colony is ruled by a king and a queen. Soldier termites defend the nest, and most of the termites are workers.

◁ **Ladybugs** are a kind of beetle. They feed on much smaller insects, called aphids and scale insects, which they find on plants. The ladybug's hard, outer wings protect the flying wings underneath.

▷ **Female mosquitoes** are bloodsuckers. They insert a needle-like tube into birds and mammals, including humans, and suck up a tiny amount of blood.

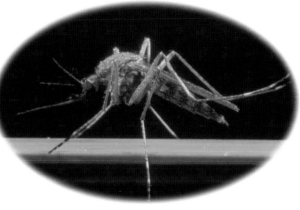

Why do wasps sting?
Wasps—and bees—mainly sting to defend themselves and their nests. Wasps also use their sting to stun or kill other insects. The sting is really a tiny tube. When it is hooked in place, the insect pumps poison down the tube.

△ **Beetles** live just about everywhere on Earth. Some live in water, and many can fly. This horned beetle is found in Borneo, in Southeast Asia.

A single bee would have to visit more than 4,000 flowers to make one tablespoon of honey. A large beehive may contain 60,000 worker bees.

ZIGZAG LADYBUG
Fold a large piece of paper backward and forward into a zigzag. Then draw a ladybug shape at one end, making sure that a part of the ladybug's body joins each edge. Cut out the ladybug, but don't cut the zigzag edges. Unfold the paper and color in all your ladybugs. You could make a chain of buzzing bees too.

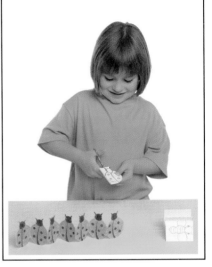

NEW WORDS
❋**abdomen** The lower or back part of an insect's body.
❋**antennae** An insect's very sensitive feelers, attached to its head.
❋**aphid** A tiny insect that feeds on plants.
❋**termite** Also called a white ant, this insect lives in a colony.
❋**thorax** The upper or front part of an insect's body, to which its wings and legs are attached.

Butterflies

Butterflies have thin, delicate wings, covered with tiny overlapping scales. These give butterflies their wonderful colors.

Like many insects, butterflies change their bodies as they develop. This change is called metamorphosis. Eggs develop into caterpillars. Each caterpillar turns into a chrysalis, and the final stage is a beautiful butterfly.

△ **Male and female butterflies** are often very different. This is a male Adonis blue butterfly. The female's wings are brown.

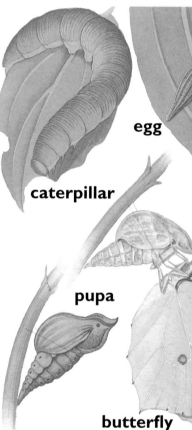

egg

caterpillar

pupa

butterfly

Butterflies are usually bright-colored and fly during the day. Most moths have much duller colors and are night-fliers.

△ **This peacock butterfly** has eyespots on its wings. These may be there to confuse or frighten a bird that might otherwise attack the insect.

▷ **A caterpillar** hatches from a butterfly egg. The caterpillar becomes a pupa, or chrysalis. A butterfly develops inside the pupa, and eventually emerges.

▷ **A hawkmoth caterpillar.** In other insects, this stage is called a larva. We call small insect larvae grubs or maggots.

The world's largest butterfly is the Queen Alexandra's birdwing, with a wingspan of more than 11 inches (28 cm).

NEW WORDS

🦋 **larva** The worm like stage of butterflies or insects after hatching.

🦋 **caterpillar** The larva of butterflies and moths.

🦋 **metamorphosis** The way insects change.

🦋 **pupa** The next stage after being a larva.

🦋 **chrysalis** A butterfly or moth pupa.

▷ **Some butterflies** and moths will travel huge distances. Often thousands and even millions of butterflies travel together. Some can even cross the Atlantic Ocean.

◁ **Unlike most moths,** the emperor moth flies by day. Females give off a strong scent, which males can pick up half a mile away.

△ **Butterflies** live almost everywhere in the world. These are found in India. Butterflies have a very keen sense of smell. They mainly use their antennae to smell, but some smell through "noses" on their feet.

BUTTERFLY OR MOTH?
When a butterfly rests, it holds its wings up. A moth folds its wings flat.

▽ **Hawkmoths** feed on nectar. They get this from flowers through their long tube-shaped tongues. Hawkmoths have large bodies and are fast fliers.

BUTTERFLY PRINTS
Fold a sheet of paper in half. Open it up and drop blobs of different-colored paints around the crease in the middle of the paper. Fold the two halves over and press the paper down. When you open it again, you will see that you have made a beautiful butterfly. When they are dry, cut your butterflies out and hang them up.

◁ **Scorpions** have a poisonous sting in their tails, which they use to paralyse prey. They also have powerful claws.

▷ **A hunting spider** from Costa Rica in, Central America. But spiders also live in cold parts of the world.

△ **Trapdoor spiders** have a very clever system for catching insects. The spider digs a burrow, lines it with silk and covers the entrance with a trapdoor. Then it lies in wait. When an insect passes nearby, the spider feels the ground move. Then it jumps out and catches the insect, quickly dragging it into its burrow.

△ **Web-making spiders** feel the silk threads of the web move when an insect is caught. They tie their prey up in a band of silk.

◁ **Garden spiders** spin beautiful circular webs. These are easily damaged, and the spiders spend a lot of time repairing them. The webs show up well when the air outside is damp.

Spiders

Spiders are similar in some ways to insects, but they belong to a different group of animals called arachnids. Scorpions, ticks, and mites are arachnids too.

Spiders have eight legs, while insects have six. Many spiders spin silky webs to catch flies and other small insects. They have fangs for seizing their prey. Most spiders paralyze their prey with poison before they kill and eat them. But only a few spiders are poisonous to humans.

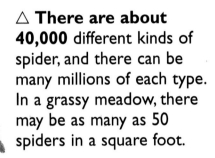

△ **There are about 40,000** different kinds of spider, and there can be many millions of each type. In a grassy meadow, there may be as many as 50 spiders in a square foot.

NEW WORDS

✴ **arachnid** A group of animals that includes spiders, scorpions, ticks, and mites.

✴ **paralyze** To make something unable to move.

✴ **spiderling** A young spider.

△ **Most spiders** and other arachnids have eight eyes. But spiders still do not see very well. They rely on touching things to know what is going on around them.

△ **A spider with its prey.** If spiders were not good hunters, the world would be overrun with insects.

◁ **Female spiders** lay up to 2,000 eggs, which they wrap in a bundle of silk threads. Spiderlings hatch from the eggs.

165

Mollusks and Crustaceans

Can squids shoot ink?
Squids and octopuses can shoot out a stream of inky fluid when they want to get away from enemies. The ink clouds the water and confuses the enemy, giving the mollusk time to escape.

Some mollusks, such as octopuses, have soft bodies. Others, such as snails, are protected by shells. Some mollusks live on land but many live in the sea.

Crustaceans get their name from their crusty covering. Most of them, such as crabs, lobsters, and shrimp, live in the sea. A few crustaceans, such as woodlice, live on land. Mollusks and crustaceans all begin life as eggs, and most of them have a larva stage.

△ **Squids** are related to octopuses. They take in water and push it out again through a funnel behind their head. This acts like a jet engine and shoots them along backward.

△ **Hermit crabs** use the shells of sea snails for protection. Some kill and eat the snail to get both a meal and a home. When it outgrows the shell, the crab looks for a new one.

The world's largest crustacean is the giant spider crab, which has a legspan of almost 13 feet (4 m).

△ **Sallylightfoot crabs** live on the rocky shores of the Galapagos Islands, off South America. As they grow, they shed their shells and grow bigger ones. These measure up to 6 inches (15 cm) across.

◁ **Octopuses** are eight-armed molluscs. Many are very small, but the largest have tentacles up to 12 feet (3.5 m) long. Octopuses can change color according to their surroundings, so they can easily hide.

△ **Lobsters** are among the largest crustaceans. They walk across the seabed on four pairs of legs.

▷ Crabs' legs are made in such a way that they can walk sideways. The front pair of legs have strong pincers which they use for picking up food. They use the back pair of legs as paddles when they swim. Most crabs live in or near the sea.

△ **A garden snail's soft body** has a muscular foot, which it uses to creep along. The snail's whole body can be pulled safely into its shell if it is threatened by another animal.

NEW WORDS

legspan The widest distance between the legs at full stretch.

shed To let something fall off.

tentacle A long bendy body part, like an arm, that is used for feeling, moving and grasping.

TREASURE CHEST

Collect some empty shells on vacation and wash them out. Paint a box and stick some shells on the lid with glue. Paint the gaps with glue and sprinkle on some sand. Glue shells around the sides of the box in patterns. When the shells are firmly stuck, brush more glue on top to varnish them. Now you can lock away all your secrets—as well as any spare shells—in your treasure chest.

Quiz

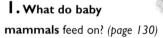
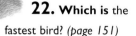

1. **What do baby mammals** feed on? *(page 130)*

2. **Where do polar bears** give birth? *(page 131)*

3. **Can you name** four kinds of apes? *(page 132)*

4. **Where do** orangutans live? *(page 133)*

5. **Which is the world's biggest** land animal? *(page 134)*

6. **What do** elephants eat? *(page 135)*

7. **Which are** the fastest cats? *(page 136)*

8. **Which big cat** likes water? *(page 137)*

9. **How long** is a blue whale? *(page 138)*

10. **What does a narwhal** have on its head? *(page 139)*

11. **What is different about bats,** compared with other mammals? *(page 140)*

12. **What do bats** use to catch insects? *(page 141)*

13. **What are** baby kangaroos called? *(page 142)*

14. **Which trees** do koalas live in? *(page 143)*

15. **Are reptiles warm-blooded** or cold-blooded? *(page 144)*

16. **Where do** emerald tree boas live? *(page 145)*

17. **What is the difference** between turtles and tortoises? *(page 146)*

18. **Where do giant** tortoises live? *(page 147)*

19. **What is a female** peafowl called? *(page 148)*

20. **Which bird** takes its name from its beautiful woven nest? *(page 149)*

21. **What do we call birds** that hunt animals for food? *(page 150)*

22. **Which is** the fastest bird? *(page 151)*

23. **What do** penguins eat? *(page 152)*

24. **Which are the largest** and the smallest penguins? *(page 153)*

25. **How do tree frogs** grip branches? *(page 154)*

26. **What are the main differences** between frogs and toads? *(page 155)*

27. **What do fish** use to breathe? *(page 157)*

28. **How do electric eels** catch their prey? *(page 157)*

29. **What happens to sharks** if they stop swimming? *(page 158)*

30. **Which is the world's** smallest shark? *(page 159)*

31. **What are the three** main parts of an insect's body? *(page 160)*

32. **What kind of insect** is a ladybug? *(page 161)*

33. **In the life cycle of a butterfly,** which stage comes after the caterpillar? *(page 162)*

34. **How are butterflies and moths different** when they rest? *(page 163)*

35. **How do garden spiders** catch insects? *(page 164)*

36. **How many legs** does a spider have? *(page 165)*

37. **Which crab steals its home** from other sea creatures? *(page 166)*

38. **Is it true** that most crabs walk sideways? *(page 167)*

Long Long Ago

The story of life on
Earth takes us right
back to the early days
of our planet. In recent times we have
learned a great deal about life's history,
including the fascinating period that we call
the Age of Dinosaurs.

For many millions of years, the land
was dominated by meat-eating and plant-
eating dinosaurs, while plesiosaurs swam
in the oceans and pterosaurs flew in the
skies. Then all these reptiles, many of them
giants, died out. They were replaced by mammals,
who gradually came to dominate the planet.
Through our study of fossils, we can now piece
together how this all came about.

Early Life

△ **This is blue-green algae,** one of the simplest forms of life, seen through a microscope. It is made up of a skin surrounding a watery "soup," and has no complicated parts.

Life on Earth has been developing and changing over billions of years. Scientists now believe that the simplest forms of life began in the world's oceans, probably over three billion years ago.

We can only guess what the very first plants and animals looked like. But we think that many early sea animals had soft bodies, without shells, bones, or other hard parts. They included jellyfish, different kinds of worms, and other creatures related to starfishes.

◁ **These jellyfish,** sea pens, and worms lived in the world's oceans about 650 million years ago. They were mainly on the seabed.

△ **The shallow coastal areas** of the early oceans were full of green, brown, and red algae, which we call seaweeds. Today, there are about 7,000 different kinds of seaweed. Most are found in warm, tropical waters.

How old are sharks?
The ancestors of today's sharks were swimming in the seas about 400 million years ago. They are one of the oldest animal groups with backbones still alive today.

△ **Fast-moving, armor-plated fish** like this Coccosteus ruled the seas about 370 million years ago. A typical Coccosteus was about 16 inches (40 cm) long, and had sharp bony ridges and tusks inside its strong jaws. It could easily catch and eat slower-moving shellfish.

The first fishes had a head, a backbone and a tail, but no fins or jaws. They could not swim fast and sucked food into their mouths instead of biting it.

▽ **Scientists** thought that Coelacanths died out about 70 million years ago. But in 1938, a fisherman caught one in the Indian Ocean. These ancient fish grow up to 6 feet (2 m) long.

171

Evolution

Most scientists believe that different forms of life on Earth developed and changed very slowly over millions of years. They call this gradual process "evolution."

Animals and plants have evolved with time, as one generation followed another. Tiny changes in one generation built up to big changes over millions of years.

As the world changed, it suited some animals better than others. Those animals which adapted easily to their surroundings did well and became more plentiful, while others died out over time.

Hyracotherium, the first horse

▽ **In 1832** Charles Darwin arrived in South America. There he found fossils of extinct animals. His studies of these and living animals led him to develop his famous theory of evolution.

NEW WORDS

adapt To adjust to different conditions.

evolution The gradual change and development of life over millions of years.

fossil Former living thing preserved in rock.

extinct Not existing any more, having died out.

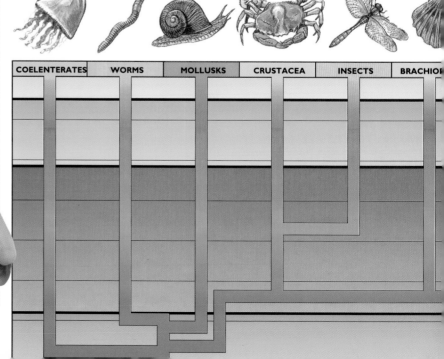

COELENTERATES	WORMS	MOLLUSKS	CRUSTACEA	INSECTS	BRACHIOR

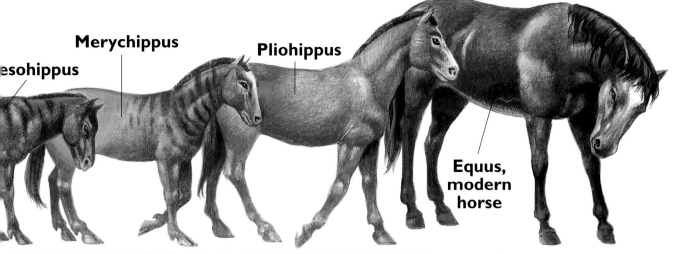

Merychippus

esohippus

Pliohippus

Equus, modern horse

△ **The horse** has developed over 50 million years. The first horse, Hyracotherium, lived in swampy forests and was as big as a modern fox. Equus has been around for about three million years.

Charles Darwin (1809-1882), the scientist, sailed around the world in a ship called *The Beagle* for five years.

△ **A giraffe** has a long neck, an anteater has a long nose, and a monkey has very long arms. All these features developed to help the animals feed and live.

▽ **This chart** shows how life has developed over millions of years. Human beings only appeared in the surprisingly recent past.

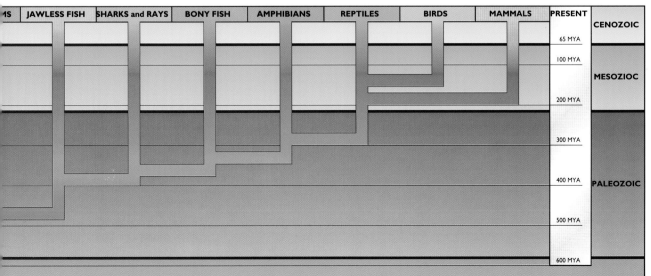

MS	JAWLESS FISH	SHARKS and RAYS	BONY FISH	AMPHIBIANS	REPTILES	BIRDS	MAMMALS	PRESENT	
									CENOZOIC
								65 MYA	
								100 MYA	
									MESOZIOC
								200 MYA	
								300 MYA	
								400 MYA	PALEOZOIC
								500 MYA	
								600 MYA	
									PRECAMBRIAN

The Age of Amphibians

About 360 million years ago, some sea creatures left the water and crawled out onto land. Already there were many different fish in the sea, as well as plants and insects on land.

By now some animals could live on land and in water. We call these animals amphibians, which means "having a double life." Steamy swamps and forests were an ideal place for them to live. Amphibians laid their eggs in water. The eggs hatched into swimming tadpoles, and when they became adults, they moved onto the land. This is exactly how amphibians such as frogs and toads live today.

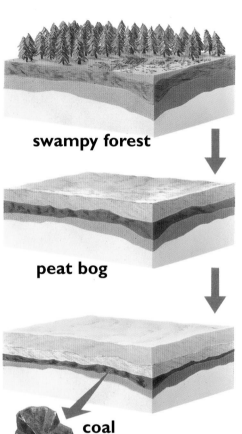

swampy forest

peat bog

coal

△ **Dead leaves** and branches formed layers of plant material in the swampy forests of the early amphibians. This made peat, and when this was covered by rocks, the pressure turned it into coal.

▷ **Ichthyostega** was one of the first amphibians. It was about 3 feet (1 m) long. Giant dragonflies and many other insects lived among the tall, treelike ferns.

◁ **Ancient coal** has provided us with knowledge about the past, as well as fuel. Some leaves survived intact as the coal was formed and made fossils like this one.

▷ **This North American bullfrog** is a good example of a modern amphibian. Bullfrogs spend most of their time near water. All frogs breathe through lungs, as well as through their skin. Today there are about 4,000 different kinds of amphibians round the world, including frogs, toads, newts, and salamanders.

Early amphibians were much bigger than they are today. The early giants died out about 200 million years ago. But there is one exception, a giant salamander, which lives in China and can grow to a length of 6 feet (1.8 m).

PREHISTORIC LANDSCAPE

Use a large cereal box as a base, with the lid as a background. Cut and tape the box, line it with blue paper, cut out a volcano and stick it on. Use tissue paper for giant ferns, and put cellophane over some blue paper for a lake. Color some sand green with food coloring and sprinkle it on the base. Build rocks with stones and cones, and add a plastic dinosaur.

NEW WORDS
amphibian An animal that lives on land but lays its eggs in water.
dragonfly An insect with a long body and two pairs of thin wings.
peat Rotted plant material in the ground.
swamp An area of wet, low and marshy ground.

Early Reptiles

Many millions of years ago, in the world's swampy forests, could be found the first reptiles. They were small, lizardlike animals, that fed mainly on insects and worms.

But reptiles are different from amphibians in one important way: reptiles can live on land all the time. Their eggs can also be laid on land, as they are protected by a leathery shell. Reptiles became the world's first true land dwellers.

Over millions of years, many different sorts of scaly-skinned reptiles evolved. Some were very large and some were small, some ate plants and some fed on other animals. At first they had legs at the sides of their bodies, like many lizards today. Later, some reptiles evolved so that their legs were more underneath their bodies, which meant they could run faster!

Which were the ruling reptiles?
The archosaurs, or "ruling reptiles," developed after the early reptiles. Some looked like crocodiles. Others could stand up on their legs, like the later dinosaurs.

Today there are about 6,500 different kinds of reptiles all over the world. These include snakes, crocodiles, alligators, lizards, and turtles.

NEW WORDS
interlock To fit in between each other.
reptile An animal with a waterproof skin covered in horny scales, who depends on its surroundings to keep warm.
yolk The yellow part inside an eggshell.

Reptiles had lost any dependance on water to lay their eggs and so they could take over the land. They could even live in hot dry deserts far from the sea.

△ **Mesosaurs** were reptiles that found their food in the sea. They went back to the water to catch fish. They had needle-like teeth that interlocked when they closed their jaws.

The first reptiles appeared about 300 million years ago. By 280 million years ago, the amphibians were becoming less common and there were many different kinds and sizes of reptiles.

The name "reptile" comes from the Latin word for "crawl."

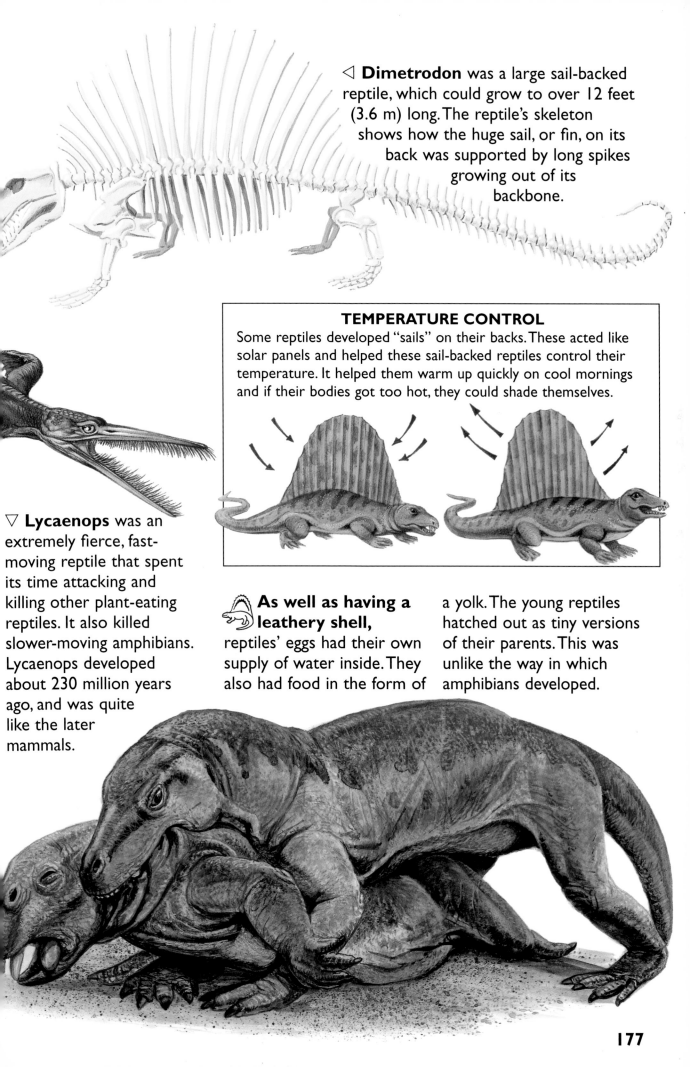

◁ **Dimetrodon** was a large sail-backed reptile, which could grow to over 12 feet (3.6 m) long. The reptile's skeleton shows how the huge sail, or fin, on its back was supported by long spikes growing out of its backbone.

TEMPERATURE CONTROL
Some reptiles developed "sails" on their backs. These acted like solar panels and helped these sail-backed reptiles control their temperature. It helped them warm up quickly on cool mornings and if their bodies got too hot, they could shade themselves.

▽ **Lycaenops** was an extremely fierce, fast-moving reptile that spent its time attacking and killing other plant-eating reptiles. It also killed slower-moving amphibians. Lycaenops developed about 230 million years ago, and was quite like the later mammals.

As well as having a leathery shell, reptiles' eggs had their own supply of water inside. They also had food in the form of a yolk. The young reptiles hatched out as tiny versions of their parents. This was unlike the way in which amphibians developed.

177

LIZARD HIPS AND BIRD HIPS

Scientists have divided dinosaurs into two main groups, according to the shapes of their hips. One group, including Tyrannosaurus (above right), had hips shaped like those of a modern lizard. The other group, which included Stegosaurus (below), had hips like a bird.

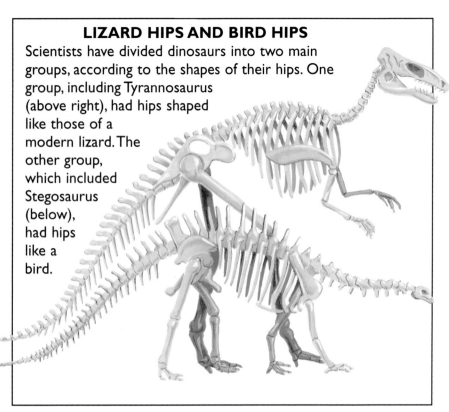

All the meat-eating dinosaurs and big four-legged plant eaters were lizard-hipped. The later bird-hipped dinosaurs were all plant eaters.

◁ **This scientist** is working at Dinosaur National Monument, Utah. More than 5,000 dinosaur fossils have been found there. The most common remains have been those of Stegosaurus.

▷ **This barrel-bodied plant-eater** used to be called Brontosaurus. But then it was found to be the same as earlier fossils called Apatosaurus, so the first name was chosen for this creature.

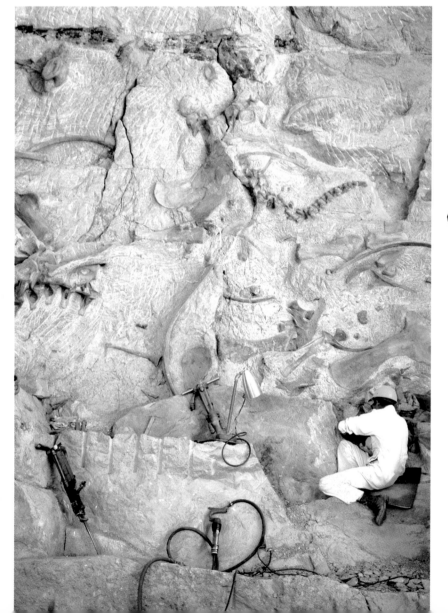

Dinosaurs

The first dinosaurs appeared on Earth about 230 million years ago. The name dinosaur means "terrible lizard," but these reptiles were only distantly related to lizards and most of them were not terrible!

For 165 million years, these amazing animals dominated the land. Some dinosaurs were huge, others were quite small. Some were meat eaters, others ate only plants. They adapted to a wide range of habitats, and could live anywhere on Earth.

◁ **The plant-eating Ultrasaurus** a huge sauropod, was the largest land animal ever to live. It was about 100 feet (30 m) long. With its long neck, it was tall enough to look over a modern three-storey house.

△ **Hundreds of dinosaur skeletons** have been collected in the badlands of Dinosaur Provincial Park, in Alberta, Canada. Rain and snow have worn away the rocks, uncovering the reptile remains. Dinosaur collectors first rushed to the area in the early 1900s.

Today's scientists move large bones from regions such as Dinosaur Provincial Park by a helicopter or truck. They put the pieces together, and the skeletons are displayed in a nearby museum.

SIZES

Dinosaurs came in all sizes. Compsognathus was a small, fast-moving, meat-eater with very sharp teeth. It was 28 inches (70 cm) to 56 inches (1.4 m) long, including its long tail. It probably ate large insects, lizards, and mouselike mammals.

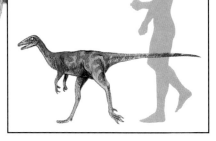

Meat-eating Dinosaurs

The dinosaur carnivores, or meat eaters, were powerfully built animals. They walked upright on their two back legs, and their shorter arms ended in hands with clawed fingers.

The big meat eaters, such as Tyrannosaurus, had a huge head on a short neck. They had very strong, sharp teeth. Nearly all meat eaters had a long, muscular tail, which they carried straight out behind them. This helped them to balance their heavy weight. Their strong back legs made meat eaters the fastest of all the dinosaurs.

△ **Oviraptor** had a tall crest on the top of its head. This birdlike creature fed on other dinosaurs' eggs which it scooped up in its three-fingered hands and cracked open with its strong jaws. Oviraptors were about 6 feet (2 m) long.

Which was fastest?
We don't know how fast dinosaurs could run, but scientists think Struthiomimus was one of the fastest. It was 13 feet (4 m) long, looked like an ostrich and may have reached speeds of 30 mph (50 km/h).

◁ **Allosaurus** was one of the biggest meat eaters before Tyrannosaurus. It was 36 feet (11 m) long. We don't know what color dinosaurs were, but some might have been brightly colored.

Ostrichlike Struthiomimus was an omnivore: it ate animals and plants. Its long claws could hook leaves and fruit from low trees. It also fed on insects and lizards.

MAKE A MEAT EATER'S TOOTH

Model a big ball of self-hardening clay into the shape of a meat-eating dinosaur's tooth. Texture the surface and mark it so that it looks ancient and fossilized. It may take up to two days for the tooth to harden. When it is hard, paint your ferocious tooth.

Baryonyx claw

Tyrannosaurus tooth

△ **Baryonyx** had long, curved thumb-claws. Tyrannosaurus had enormous teeth. They were up to 7 inches (18 cm) long, with sharp edges like steak knives. Tooth finds have helped to tell us what different dinosaurs fed on.

The Age of the Dinosaurs is divided into three periods: the Triassic (240-205 million years ago), the Jurassic (205-138 million years ago) and the Cretaceous period (138-65 million years ago).

▷ **Tyrannosaurus** was about 40 feet (12 m) long and weighed over 6 tons. Its forward-facing eyes helped it to judge distance well as it moved in to attack smaller dinosaurs. Its tiny arms look feeble but held sharp claws.

Plant-eating Dinosaurs

Which had the longest neck?
Mamenchisaurus, a huge plant eater found in China, had the longest neck of any animal ever known. Its neck was 50 feet (15 m) long—longer than eight tall men lying head to toe!

The dinosaur herbivores, or plant eaters, fed on the vegetation they could reach. Small herbivores ate roots and plants on the ground, and others may have reared up on their back legs to reach higher leaves.

The long-necked sauropods, such as Diplodocus, were tall enough to reach the treetops. These huge animals must have spent nearly all their time eating.

NEW WORDS
herbivore A vegetarian animal that eats only plants.
rear up To raise itself on its back legs.
stud A curved lump or knob.
vegetation Living plants, including twigs and the leaves of trees.

Scutellosaurus was a tiny plant eater, about the size of a modern cat. It had rows of bony studs along its back and tail, to protect it from attack by any larger meat eaters. It could walk or run on its back legs, as well as on all fours.

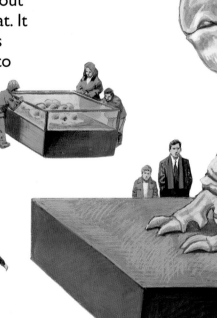

IGUANODON

This large, heavy dinosaur was a peaceful plant eater that could stand and walk either on its back legs or on all fours. It had spiked thumbs, which it may have used to defend itself if it was attacked by a hungry meat eater.

◁ **Long-necked plant eaters** may also have reared up to reach even higher treetops. Diplodocus picked leaves off with its front teeth, but had no back teeth for chewing.

The huge shoulder bones of Ultrasaurus were 9 feet (2.7 m) long, much longer than the tallest human. Its hip bones were also bigger than a man. Ultrasaurus was about 100 feet (30 m) long.

DIG UP A DIPLODOCUS

Cut up straws for bones and make them into a complete skeleton on a cardboard base. Brush each straw with glue and fix them firmly into position. Leave the straws to dry, and then brush more glue between the bones and around the whole skeleton. Sprinkle all over with sand. After a few minutes, tip the surplus sand onto newspaper. Then you'll have your very own fossilized Diplodocus!

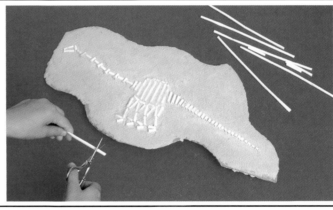

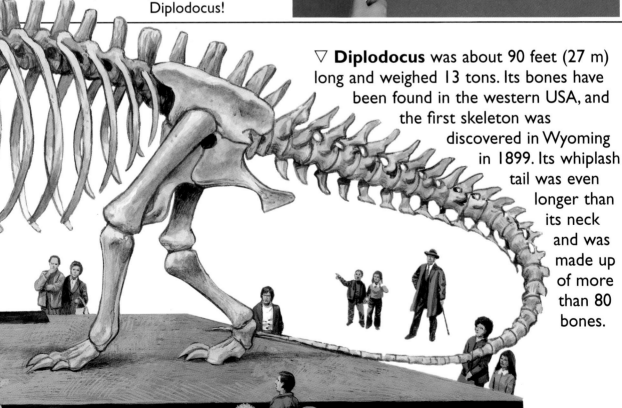

▽ **Diplodocus** was about 90 feet (27 m) long and weighed 13 tons. Its bones have been found in the western USA, and the first skeleton was discovered in Wyoming in 1899. Its whiplash tail was even longer than its neck and was made up of more than 80 bones.

Warm-or Cold-Blooded Creatures?

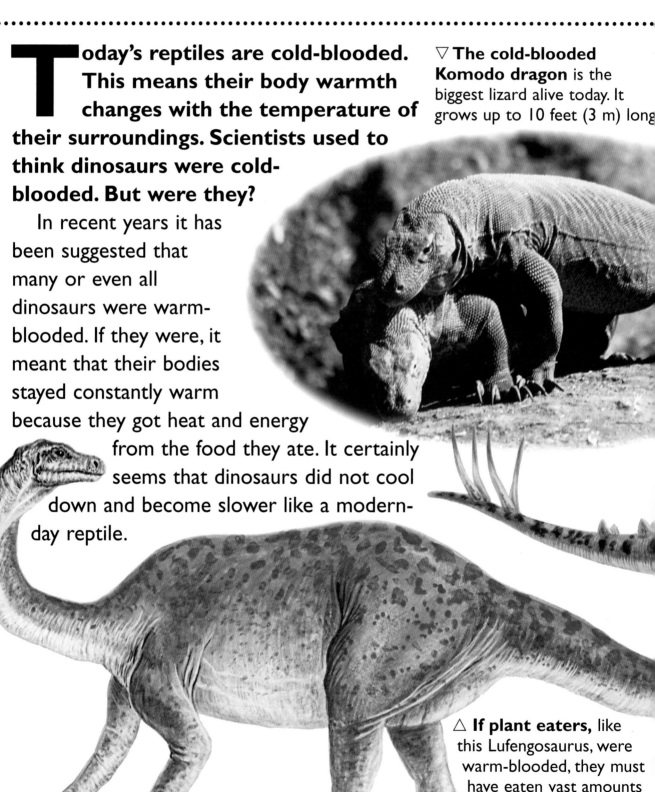

Today's reptiles are cold-blooded. This means their body warmth changes with the temperature of their surroundings. Scientists used to think dinosaurs were cold-blooded. But were they?

In recent years it has been suggested that many or even all dinosaurs were warm-blooded. If they were, it meant that their bodies stayed constantly warm because they got heat and energy from the food they ate. It certainly seems that dinosaurs did not cool down and become slower like a modern-day reptile.

▽ **The cold-blooded Komodo dragon** is the biggest lizard alive today. It grows up to 10 feet (3 m) long

△ **If plant eaters,** like this Lufengosaurus, were warm-blooded, they must have eaten vast amounts of food. Or perhaps they were cold-blooded?

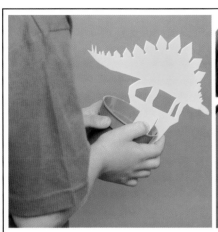

CATCH A DINOSAUR GAME
Cut dinosaur shapes out of cardboard. Make slits to fit the dinosaurs onto plastic pots. Put sand in the pots to make them stable. Then throw a ball into a pot to catch a dinosaur.

Cold-blooded reptiles have to wait for the sun to warm them up each morning before they can move about. This puts them in danger.

A cold-blooded Komodo dragon needs its own weight in food every two months. A warm-blooded lion needs its own weight in food every week. Warm-blooded animals need to eat more food so that they can keep warm.

Some scientists say that the long-necked dinosaurs must have been warm-blooded, because they would need such high blood pressure to get the blood up to their brain.

△ **Plated dinosaurs** such as Tuojiangosaurus may have used the bony plates on their back to soak up the sun's heat and warm themselves up. So they may have been cold-blooded.

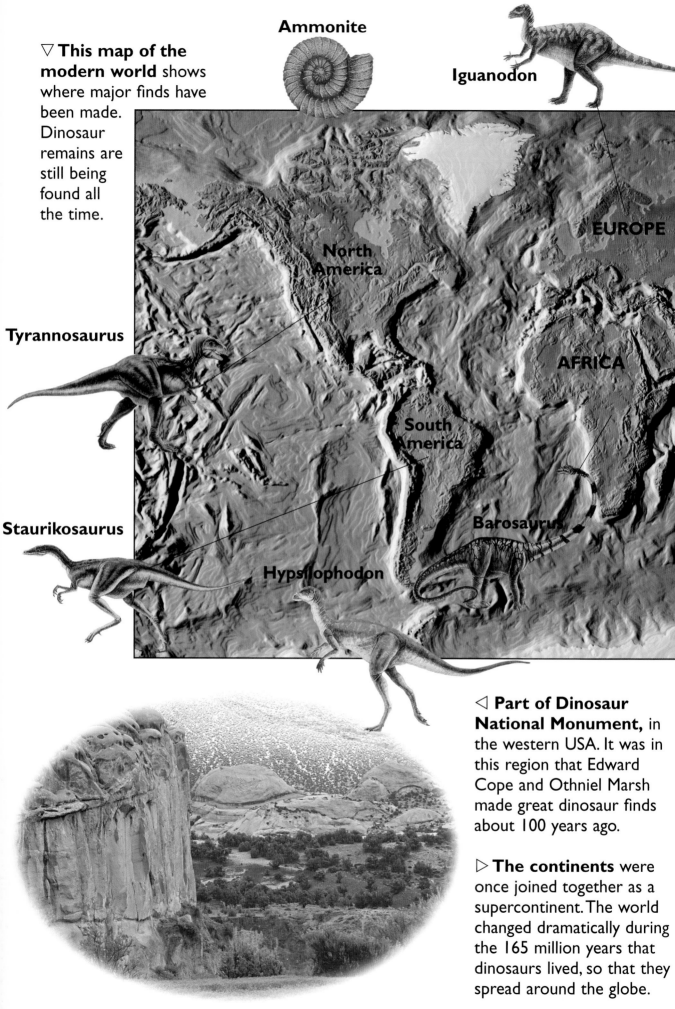

▽ **This map of the modern world** shows where major finds have been made. Dinosaur remains are still being found all the time.

Ammonite

Iguanodon

EUROPE

North America

AFRICA

Tyrannosaurus

South America

Staurikosaurus

Barosaurus

Hypsilophodon

◁ **Part of Dinosaur National Monument,** in the western USA. It was in this region that Edward Cope and Othniel Marsh made great dinosaur finds about 100 years ago.

▷ **The continents** were once joined together as a supercontinent. The world changed dramatically during the 165 million years that dinosaurs lived, so that they spread around the globe.

186

Where Dinosaurs Lived

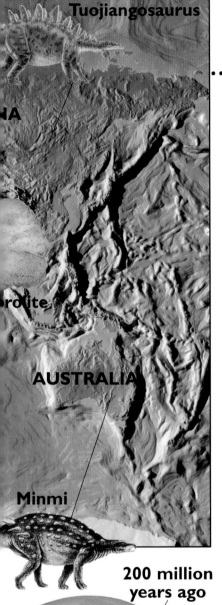

Tuojiangosaurus

...A

...rolite

AUSTRALIA

Minmi

Dinosaur remains have been found all over the world. In fact, similar dinosaurs have been found on different continents, yet we know that they were land animals and could not have swum across vast oceans.

During the Age of Dinosaurs the continents were slowly drifting apart from the original supercontinent. So the dinosaurs could have crossed from one continent to another by land early on.

NEW WORDS
Coprolites Fossilized animal droppings.
supercontinent The huge mass of land that once existed. The individual continents split off from this mass.

200 million years ago

100 million years ago

Today

▽ **Famous dinosaur collectors:** 1 Dr Robert Plot; 2 Mary Mantell; 3 Dr. Gideon Mantell; 4 Sir Richard Owen; 5 Edward Cope; 6 Othniel Marsh.

5

1

6

3

4

2

Moving Herds

We have learned a lot about how dinosaurs lived from the discovery of fossil footprints. These show how dinosaurs moved, and whether they traveled alone, in small groups, or in larger herds.

Apatosaurus was one of the large plant eaters. From footprints found in Texas, we know that these dinosaurs roamed across the North American plains in herds. The footprints were all made at the same time, 150 million years ago.

Herds of up to 100 plant-eaters may have traveled long distances in search of food. Some tracks have shown that smaller and younger dinosaurs walked in the middle of the herd, so that they were safe from any attack.

MAKING FOOTPRINTS

Pour paint into a baking tin or something similar. Put this at one end of some spread-out newspapers, and put a bucket of water and a towel at the other end. Then step into the paint, walk across the paper, and wash your feet in the water. Ask a friend to do the same, so that you can compare prints.

△ **These dinosaur tracks** were found in Queensland, Australia. At the time of the dinosaurs, the continent of Australia was moving away from Antarctica.

▽ **Dinosaurs** such as Parasaurolophus and Saurolophus had head balloons and crests. They may have used these to increase the noises they made to warn other herd members.

▽ **A herd of Apatosaurus** on the move. For many years, most scientists thought that these dinosaurs lived in water, using their long neck like a snorkel. The footprint finds proved this to be quite wrong.

Scientists think that Apatosaurus may have been able to travel at a similar speed to modern elephants. But a huge Brachiosaurus probably only moved at a slow walk of about 3 mph (5 km/h) or so.

▽ **Hypsilophodon** were small, fast plant eaters. Remains of herds have been found. The first known Hypsilophodon was found in 1849, but at that time it was wrongly thought to be a common Iguanodon.

NEW WORDS
crest A bony bump on top of a dinosaur's head; some crests were big and might have been used in signaling.

head balloon A flap of skin on top of a dinosaur's head, that blew up just like a balloon.

MOVING AROUND
The Tarbosaurus found in China is so similar to the Tyrannosaurus found in North America that they must be very close relatives. Perhaps they simply travelled in different directions.

Tarbosaurus

Tyrannosaurus

189

Eggs and Nests

Female dinosaurs laid eggs, just like modern reptiles. The eggs were leathery and hard-shelled, which gave them protection. They were often laid in mud nests or hollows. Then the mothers covered them with plants or sand.

We know all this from the fossilized eggs that have been found. The first of these was discovered in the Gobi Desert in Mongolia in 1923. We also know that some groups of dinosaurs built their nests close together, in colonies. Scientists think that some dinosaurs returned to the same nesting place year after year. Some dinosaur mothers stayed by their nests to look after the eggs and the new baby dinosaurs.

Male and female dinosaurs may have looked different, especially in their coloring. Two slightly different kinds of the same dinosaur have been found. These might have been male and female.

△ **These tiny Protoceratops** are hatching from their eggs. Their mother is close by, and she may have stayed to help feed and protect her young until they were able to fend for themselves - about 80 million years ago.

MAKE A NEST OF EGGS

First roll self-hardening clay into oval egg shapes, and then let them dry. If you want to make a really big dinosaur egg, crush old newspaper into a ball before covering it with clay and smearing any joins together with water. Mold the clay into an egg shape and let it dry. Then you could paint the eggs whatever color you think they might have been. Finally, when the paint is dry, put your dinosaur eggs together in a nest made of sand.

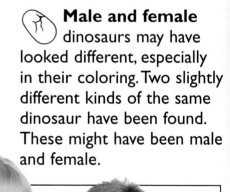

◁ **Today's crocodiles** behave in a way which is probably very similar to dinosaurs. They make nests and cover them over with plants and mud, which help keep the eggs warm. When the babies hatch, mother carries them gently in her jaws to a nearby pool.

How big?

The biggest dinosaur eggs found so far were 12 inches (30 cm) long— only about six times bigger than a chicken's egg. The rapid growth of hatched babies is a reason to think that dinosaurs were warm-blooded.

NEW WORDS

hatch To break out of an egg.

colony A group of animals who live together.

leathery Tough and flexible, like animal skin.

▽ **Maiasaura,** which means "good mother lizard," was so named when a group of its nests were found with fossilized eggs, and some babies, still inside them. The mothers would have scooped out mud nests about 6 feet (2 m) across and laid up to 20 eggs inside, each about 20 cm long. They then covered the eggs up.

191

Helmets, Spines, and Armor

Big, slow-moving animals need to protect themselves against fast, fierce meat eaters. Many plant-eating dinosaurs had some form of armor-plating to offer this protection.

Some dinosaurs had plates and spines running down their back and tail. Others had spikes that grew in their skin. They even had a bony club at the end of their tail, which was a powerful weapon against attackers. One group of dinosaurs had thick, bony skulls, which they used to head-butt each other during fights.

△ **The largest** bone-headed dinosaur, Pachycephalosaurus, had a thick, dome-shaped skull. This head-butting creature was 15 feet (4.6 m) long.

Styracosaurus lived on Earth about 75 million years ago, and fossils have been found in the USA and Canada.

Triceratops' teeth were hard on one side. The other, softer side wore down faster, leaving a sharp cutting edge.

Stegosaurus was about 30 feet (9 m) long, but it had a small head and its brain was little bigger than a walnut. Dinosaur skulls were filled mainly with muscle and bone.

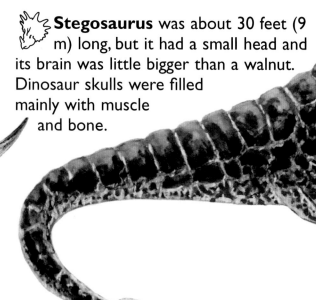

△ **Styracosaurus** had long spikes sticking out of a bony frill. It also had a large nose horn, like a modern rhinoceros.

CARDBOARD STEGOSAURUS

Cut the sides off some large cardboard boxes and tape them together. Draw the long dinosaur body shape of a Stegosaurus (see the photograph, right) and cut it out. Make plates and tail spikes from cardboard, and use egg cups for scales. Paint the egg cups green and stick them on the body. Fasten the plates with tape. Crush up lots of pieces of tissue paper and glue them all over your dinosaur's body. You could use a bottle top for a beady, prehistoric eye!

◁ **Triceratops** means "three-horned face." Although the horns were for self-defence, scientists think that these dinosaurs may also have fought one another.

△ **Euoplocephalus** had slabs of bony armor, spikes on its back, and a clubbed tail. It used its powerful muscles to swing its tail at any enemies.

Other Giant Reptiles

During the long Age of Dinosaurs, other giant reptiles lived in the world's oceans.

Like their dinosaur cousins, sea reptiles breathed air. This meant that they had to come to the surface regularly to fill their lungs. Sea reptiles such as the plesiosaurs and pliosaurs might have laid their eggs in sandy nests on the shore. Although they, too, were reptiles, ichthyosaurs gave birth to live young at sea.

All these giant reptiles died out, but smaller crocodiles and turtles still exist today.

NEW WORDS
plesiosaur A sea reptile with a long neck and limbs like paddles.
pliosaur A sea reptile with a large head and a short neck.
ichthyosaur A streamlined sea reptile shaped a bit like a modern dolphin.

▽ **Tanystrophaeus** was a land animal, but it used its long, thin neck to catch fish underwater. Shonisaurus was the largest ichthyosaur, growing up to 50 feet (15 m) long.

Tanystrophaeus

Shonisaurus

▽ **Elasmosaurus** was about 43 feet (13 m) in length, making it the longest of the long-necked plesiosaurs. Kronosaurus was a huge pliosaur with massive, sharp teeth. And Archelon was a giant turtle, almost 13 feet (4 m) long. All three sea reptiles lived toward the end of the Age of Dinosaurs.

Their air-filled lungs made it very difficult for plesiosaurs to dive deep under water to catch their prey. To weigh themselves down and make things easier, they seem to have swallowed stones. Crocodiles do exactly the same today.

△ **Deinosuchus** was the largest crocodile that ever lived. It was up to 40 feet (12 m) long and had massive jaws. It swam in rivers and swamps, and might have fed on land animals coming there to drink.

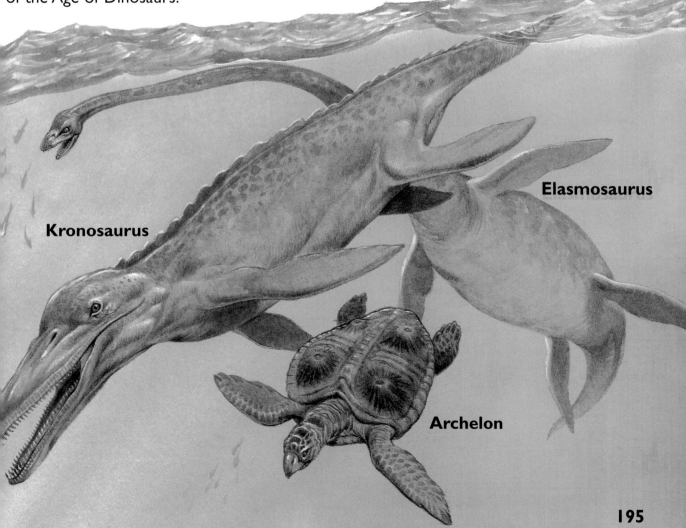

Kronosaurus

Elasmosaurus

Archelon

Into the Air

Reptiles took to the air over 200 million years ago. While dinosaurs ruled the land, pterosaurs controlled the skies long before the first birds took off.

Pterosaurs flew on wings of skin, which stretched out from their bodies, along their arms to their long fingers. They launched themselves from high cliffs and flapped their wings as they rode the air currents. They had light, delicate bones, which made it easier for them to stay in the air.

▽ **Pteranodons** flew over the seas and used their long, toothless beaks to catch fish. They had a wing span of more than 16 feet (5 m). The long bony crest at the back of their heads may have been used as a rudder, to guide and balance them as they flew.

Fossils of Pteranodon have been dated at about 80 million years old.

EARLY GLIDERS

Icarosaurus and Coelurosauravus were early lizardlike animals with wings. Icarosaurus lived over 200 million years ago. It climbed trees, with its wings folded against its body. Then it launched itself off, and its thin wings helped it glide through the air

Icarosaurus

Coelurosauravus

NEW WORDS

glide To travel through the air using natural air currents instead of wing-power.

pterosaur A flying reptile that existed at the same time as the dinosaurs.

rudder Something that helps in steering.

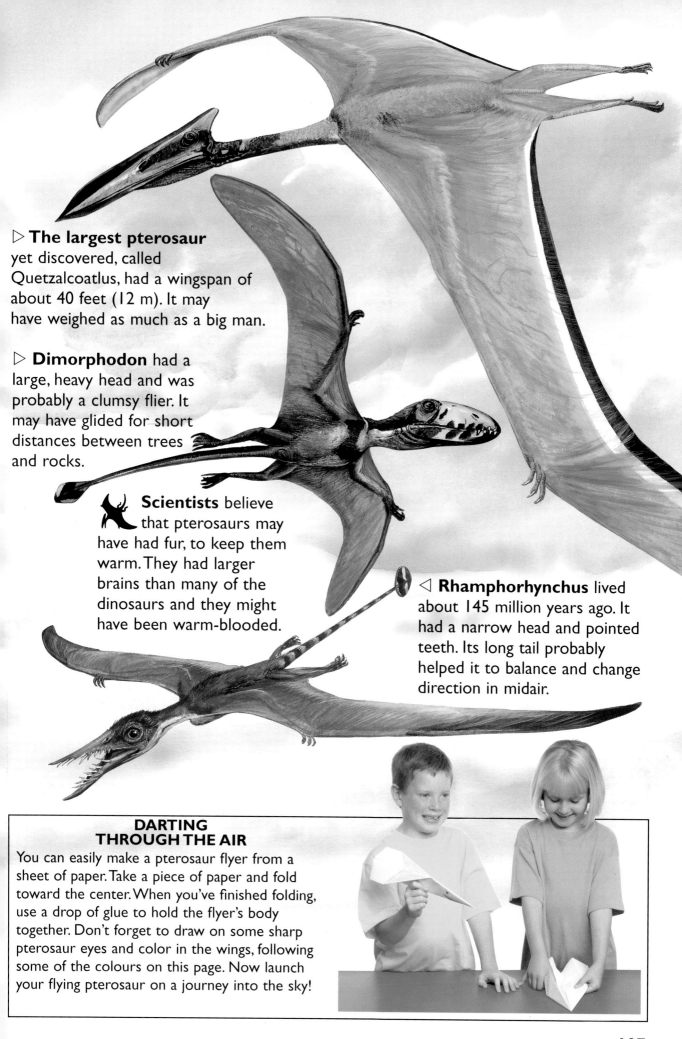

▷ **The largest pterosaur** yet discovered, called Quetzalcoatlus, had a wingspan of about 40 feet (12 m). It may have weighed as much as a big man.

▷ **Dimorphodon** had a large, heavy head and was probably a clumsy flier. It may have glided for short distances between trees and rocks.

Scientists believe that pterosaurs may have had fur, to keep them warm. They had larger brains than many of the dinosaurs and they might have been warm-blooded.

◁ **Rhamphorhynchus** lived about 145 million years ago. It had a narrow head and pointed teeth. Its long tail probably helped it to balance and change direction in midair.

DARTING THROUGH THE AIR

You can easily make a pterosaur flyer from a sheet of paper. Take a piece of paper and fold toward the center. When you've finished folding, use a drop of glue to hold the flyer's body together. Don't forget to draw on some sharp pterosaur eyes and color in the wings, following some of the colours on this page. Now launch your flying pterosaur on a journey into the sky!

The First Birds

The first known bird lived about 150 million years ago. Scientists think that it was closely related to the dinosaurs, and in many ways it was very much like a reptile.

We call this first bird Archaeopteryx, which means "ancient wing." Unlike the pterosaurs, Archaeopteryx's body was covered with feathers. But scientists think it might not have been able to fly very well.

Around 90 million years ago, while dinosaurs still roamed the land, water birds were starting to catch fish in the sea. Some of these flying creatures may still have been more at home in the water than they were on land or in the air.

What colour?

We don't know what color the first birds were. Fossil feathers show us shape and size, but not color. Males and females may have been different colors.

△ **Diatryma** was a fast-running flightless bird with a large, parrotlike beak and big claws. It was as big as a tall human and lived about 50 million years ago. Diatryma might have chased the first small horses.

▽ **Hesperornis** was a good underwater swimmer, but probably couldn't fly. Ichthyornis was like a modern gull and could fly to catch fish.

Hesperornis

Ichthyornis

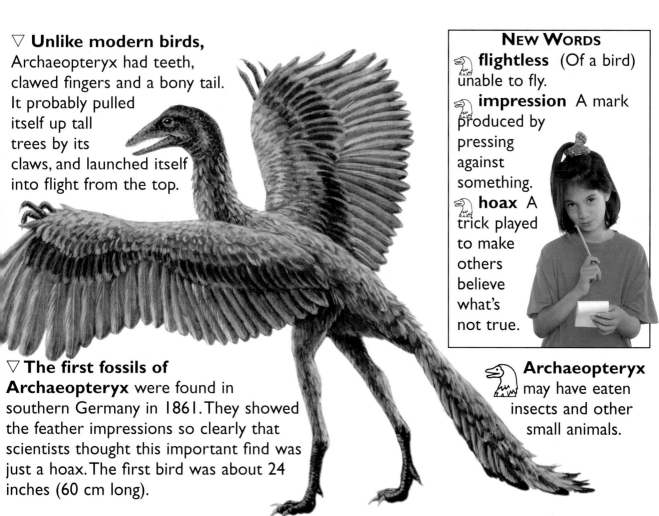

▽ **Unlike modern birds,**
Archaeopteryx had teeth,
clawed fingers and a bony tail.
It probably pulled
itself up tall
trees by its
claws, and launched itself
into flight from the top.

NEW WORDS
🦅 **flightless** (Of a bird) unable to fly.
🦅 **impression** A mark produced by pressing against something.
🦅 **hoax** A trick played to make others believe what's not true.

▽ **The first fossils of Archaeopteryx** were found in southern Germany in 1861. They showed the feather impressions so clearly that scientists thought this important find was just a hoax. The first bird was about 24 inches (60 cm long).

🦅 **Archaeopteryx** may have eaten insects and other small animals.

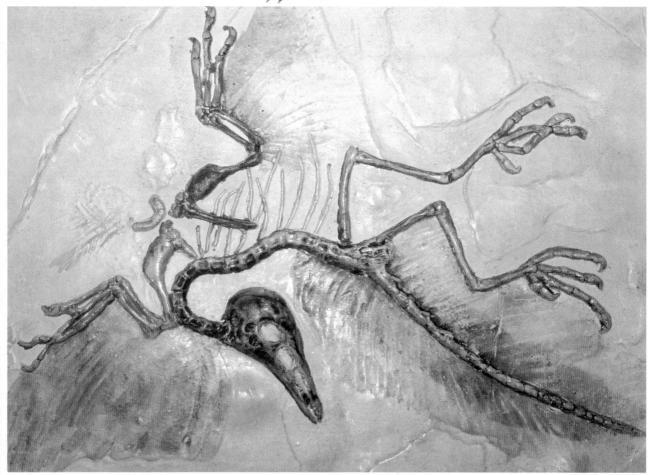

▷ **This is Meteor Crater,** in Arizona. It is over a half a mile (1 km) across and was made about 50,000 years ago when a meteorite hit Earth. Some scientists think a much bigger asteroid might have struck Earth 65 million years ago.

A huge crashing meteorite could have caused the dust that blocked out the Sun and killed the dinosaurs.

Did all the eggs disappear?
Another theory is that small mammals raided dinosaur nests and ate so many eggs all at once that there were no more dinosaur babies. This seems an unlikely story.

NEW WORDS
asteroid A tiny or minor planet.
erupt To throw out rocks, gases, and other material.
meteorite A rocklike object from space that hits the Earth.

▷ **If we had not found fossilized bones,** we would not even know that dinosaurs ever existed.

▽ **It could be that many vast volcanoes** erupted over a period of a few years or even longer. This might have made the Earth too hot, poisoned the air and blotted out the Sun.

Dinosaurs Die Out

Dinosaurs became extinct, or died out, about 65 million years ago. The great reptiles of the sea and air disappeared at the same time. We are not sure why this happened.

It could be that at that time the Earth became covered in dust and smoke, blocking out sunlight for months or even years. Plants and many animals, including dinosaurs, could not have survived this catastrophe.

▽ **Plant eaters** such as Saltasaurus (below) and meat eaters like Tyrannosaurus, were among the last known dinosaurs. The meat eaters ran out of food once the plant eaters had died out!

Mammals Take Ove[r]

The first mammals appeared about 200 million years ago. During the time that dinosaurs ruled the land, mammals remained very small.

Most early mammals probably stayed in burrows during the day, coming out to feed at night when larger animals were asleep. But when the dinosaurs died out, the warm-blooded mammals took over the land. They grew bigger and more powerful, and some became fierce meat eaters.

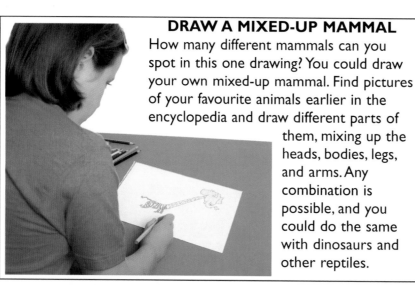

△ **Today's common tree shrew** is probably quite similar to the very early mammals that existed in the time of the dinosaurs. Shrews are still found in most parts of the world.

DRAW A MIXED-UP MAMMAL

How many different mammals can you spot in this one drawing? You could draw your own mixed-up mammal. Find pictures of your favourite animals earlier in the encyclopedia and draw different parts of them, mixing up the heads, bodies, legs, and arms. Any combination is possible, and you could do the same with dinosaurs and other reptiles.

▽ **This scene** shows what the world might have looked like about 40 million years ago. Mammals like today's elephants, bears, horses, and bats were starting to rule the land and compete with each other.

▷ **Morganucodon** (above, right) and Deltatheridium (below) were small, very early mammals. It's easy to see why we compare them to modern shrews.

Uintatherium was an enormous mammal, rather like today's bulky rhinoceros. It was about 13 feet (4 m) long and had six big, hornlike bony knobs on its head. The males also had large tusks, which they may have used for fighting and for self-defense.

△ **Pantolambda** was an early hoofed plant eater, about the size of a modern sheep. There were new grasses on the plains, but it may have spent some of its time wallowing around in the mud, just like a modern-day hippopotamus.

Early Man

Human like creatures that we call "southern apes" lived in Africa about four million years ago. We know that about two million years later, a kind of human that we call "handy man" was making and using stone tools.

Hundreds of thousands of years after that, "upright man" found out how to use fire. Next came Neanderthal man. He evolved about 250,000 years ago and died out about 30,000 years ago. He was the predecessor of "modern man," or Homo sapiens, which means "wise man." He evolved successfully, and developed farming, kept animals and made cave paintings. These were our human ancestors.

▽ **Prehistoric paintings** in caves at Lascaux, France, were found by four teenage boys in 1940. The paintings, of animals were made about 17,000 years ago.

△ **We think that Homo erectus,** or "upright man," was the first to use fire. This was useful for cooking food, keeping warm and scaring animals away from shelters such as caves. Hot stones may also have been used to make simple ovens.

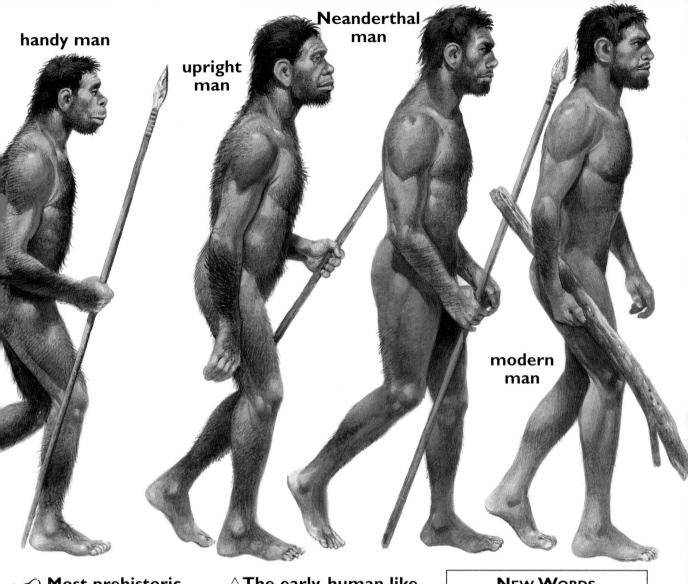

handy man

upright man

Neanderthal man

modern man

🐂 **Most prehistoric people** were hunters and gatherers. They would hunt large animals such as mammoths and woolly rhinoceroses. They would gather fruits, berries, and seeds too.

△ **The early, human like** "southern ape" was called Australopithecus. Next came "handy man" (Homo habilis), who could make stone tools, then "upright man," who used fire. We modern humans are from the group called "wise man" (Homo sapiens).

STONE PAINTINGS
You can turn a collection of smooth pebbles or stones into a friendly snake. Give your stones a good wash and then let them dry thoroughly before you start painting. Use the biggest stone for the head, and then go down in size all the way to the tip of the tail. Paint the body of your snake with green poster paint, and let this dry before adding yellow markings, a pair of eyes and a forked tongue. When the stones are dry, arrange them into a slithering snake shape.

Discovering Dinosaurs

The dinosaurs died out many millions of years before the first humans walked on Earth. When people first found dinosaur bones and fossils, they didn't know what they were.

Less than 200 years ago, scientists realized that these were extinct reptiles, and in 1841 Sir Richard Owen gave them the name "dinosaurs." Since then scientists called paleontologists have studied many thousands of fossils carefully. They have put together the picture of prehistoric life that we have today.

△ **Some prehistoric insects** were trapped in amber, made from a sticky substance that oozes from the trunks of some trees and hardens.

Dinosaurs' names are usually given in Latin. Many of their names describe the particular animal's appearance. So Euoplocephalus means "well-armored head."

▽ **When dinosaurs died,** their bones were covered in mud. This hardened into rock when more layers built up on top. Then over millions of years the rock wore away again to reveal fossilized bones.

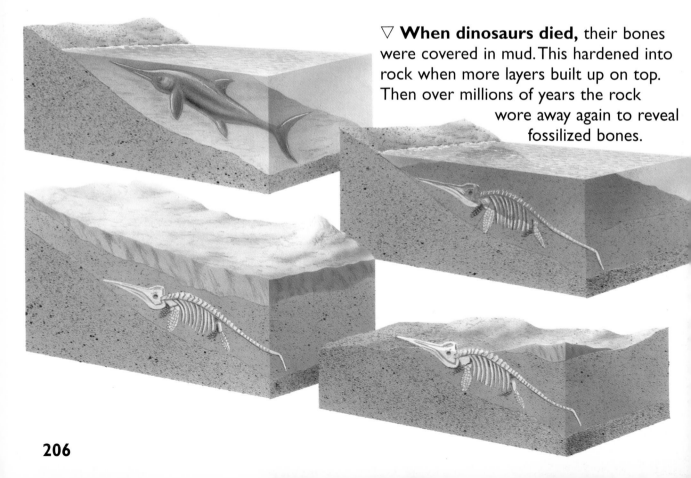

▷ **These bones of a Hypacrosaurus,** plant eater, show the shape of the animal very clearly. The bones are usually found near each other, but often have to be put together like a jigsaw puzzle.

▽ **First dirt has to be brushed** from bones. Then each bone is labeled and given a number. This helps when putting the pieces together later.

▽ **Paleontologists** keep detailed notes on where bones were found. They take photographs and make drawings and diagrams before the bones are taken away from the original site. Other scientists can learn a lot from these original notes.

▽ **Bones are carefully wrapped** in wet plaster before they are moved from the original site. When the plaster has hardened, the bones can safely be taken to a laboratory. The plaster jacket that protected them can then be taken off, so that scientists can test and study the bones.

NEW WORDS

laboratory The place where a scientist works and does experiments.

paleontologist A scientist who studies fossils.

plaster A soft paste that hardens when it is left to dry.

Quiz

1. **What shape** is a starfish? *(page 170)*

2. **How many different kinds** of seaweed are there? *(page 171)*

3. **Which famous scientist** traveled to South America in 1832? *(page 172)*

4. **What was the name** of Charles Darwin's ship? *(page 173)*

5. **Where do amphibians** lay their eggs? *(page 174)*

6. **Which is the largest amphibian** alive today? *(page 175)*

7. **What does the name reptile** come from? *(page 176)*

8. **What did sail-backed reptiles** use their sail for? *(page 177)*

9. **Which animals** are the two types of dinosaur hips named after? *(page 178)*

10. **When did the first dinosaurs** appear on Earth? *(page 179)*

11. **What was the name** of an egg-snatching dinosaur? *(page 180)*

12. **Which period** comes after the Jurassic? *(page 181)*

13. **What is** a herbivore? *(page 182)*

14. **How long** was Diplodocus? *(page 183)*

15. **Which is the biggest** lizard alive today? *(page 184)*

16. **What warms reptiles** up each morning? *(page 185)*

17. **Where did the famous dinosaur** collectors Cope and Marsh make great finds? *(page 186)*

18. **What do we call the huge mass** of land that the continents split from? *(page 187)*

19. **Why did young dinosaurs** walk in the middle of the herd? *(page 188)*

20. **What did footprints** tell us about Apatosaurus? *(page 189)*

21. **Where were the first dinosaur** eggs found? *(page 190)*

22. **What does the name** "Maiasaura" mean? *(page 191)*

23. **What was special** about Pachycephalosaurus' head? *(page 192)*

24. **Which dinosaur** had a "three-horned face"? *(page 193)*

25. **Which had a longer neck,** a plesiosaur or a pliosaur? *(page 194)*

26. **What did plesiosaurs swallow** to weigh them down? *(page 195)*

27. **Did pterosaurs have** feathers? *(page 196)*

28. **How big was the wingspan** of the largest pterosaur? *(page 197)*

29. **When did** the first bird live? *(page 198)*

30. **What did Archaeopteryx** use its claws for? *(page 199)*

31. **Where is** Meteor Crater? *(page 200)*

32. **When did** dinosaurs die out? *(page 201)*

33. **Which modern animal** is similar to the very early mammals? *(page 202)*

34. **What did Uintatherium** have on its head? *(page 203)*

35. **Who do we think** was first to use fire? *(page 204)*

36. **Which came first,** "upright man" or "handy man"? *(page 205)*

37. **Were there humans alive** at the same time as dinosaurs? *(page 206)*

38. **What do scientists wrap** dinosaur bones in? *(page 207)*

People and Places

The people of the world live on six different continents. Each of these continents has its own special landscapes and famous places, all of which have developed in their own unique way throughout history. Humans live in rain forests and deserts, near oceans and rivers, in small villages as well as gigantic, crowded cities.

All the world's people belong to the same human race, despite being split up into hundreds of nations and other groups. Many of these groups have their own language, religion, festivals, and customs, all based on their own special history. We can all learn by studying how other people live, all over the world.

North America

◁ **The Grand Canyon,** in Arizona, is the largest gorge in the world. It is about 210 miles (350 km) long and 1.2 miles (2 km) deep.

The continent of North America stretches all the way from the frozen Arctic Ocean in the north to the warm waters of the Caribbean Sea in the south. It includes two of the biggest countries in the world, Canada and the United States of America.

The land varies from the freezing icecaps of Greenland to the huge cold forests of Canada, from the American prairies and the deserts of northern Mexico, to the tropical rain forests of Central America. The Rocky Mountains run almost all the way down the western side of the continent, while New York City—the largest city in the United States—is on the eastern side.

NEW WORDS
📖 **arc** A curved shape.
📖 **borough** A district or part of a city.
📖 **gorge** A deep valley with steep sides.
📖 **icecap** A permanent covering of ice in a region.
📖 **prairie** A large area of flat grassland.

▽ **The skyscraper city** of New York. The crowded island of Manhattan, one of the city's five boroughs, is surrounded by three rivers. Bridges and tunnels link it with the rest of the city.

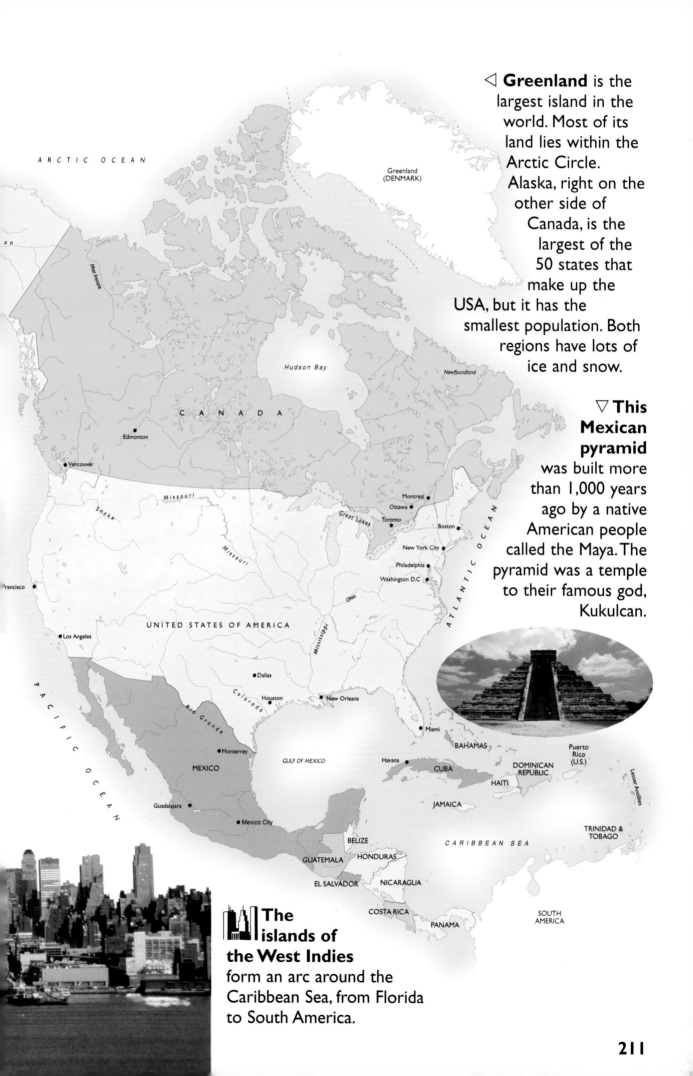

ARCTIC OCEAN

Greenland
(DENMARK)

◁ **Greenland** is the largest island in the world. Most of its land lies within the Arctic Circle. Alaska, right on the other side of Canada, is the largest of the 50 states that make up the USA, but it has the smallest population. Both regions have lots of ice and snow.

Mackenzie

Hudson Bay

Newfoundland

C A N A D A

Edmonton

Vancouver

Missouri

Snake

Missouri

Montreal
Ottawa
Great Lakes
Toronto
Boston
New York City
Philadelphia
Washington D.C

▽ **This Mexican pyramid** was built more than 1,000 years ago by a native American people called the Maya. The pyramid was a temple to their famous god, Kukulcan.

Francisco

Ohio

Los Angeles

UNITED STATES OF AMERICA

Mississippi

ATLANTIC OCEAN

P
A
C
I
F
I
C

O
C
E
A
N

Dallas

Colorado

Houston

New Orleans

Rio Grande

Miami

BAHAMAS

Puerto Rico
(U.S.)

Monterrey

GULF OF MEXICO

Havana

CUBA

DOMINICAN
REPUBLIC

Lesser Antilles

MEXICO

HAITI

Guadalajara

JAMAICA

Mexico City

TRINIDAD &
TOBAGO

BELIZE

CARIBBEAN SEA

GUATEMALA
HONDURAS

EL SALVADOR
NICARAGUA

COSTA RICA

SOUTH
AMERICA

PANAMA

The islands of the West Indies form an arc around the Caribbean Sea, from Florida to South America.

211

North American People

△ **The Inuit** live in the very north of the continent, in northern Canada and Greenland. In their own language, Inuit just means people.

Many thousands of years ago, hunters from northeast Asia crossed a land bridge to the region that is now called Alaska. These native people gradually spread southward, across the whole of the continent.

About 1,000 years ago, Viking explorers sailed to North America from Europe. But it was less than 500 years ago that Europeans first made permanent settlements there.

Today, the USA forms a single nation with its own way of life, but it is made up of people who came to live there from all over the world. This is what we call a "multi-cultural society."

◁ **Riding a bucking bronco** is one of the tests a cowboy has to go through at a rodeo. The cowboy tries to stay on the horse for as long as he can.

Years ago, cowboys drove huge herds of cattle to railroad towns. This was a hard life and not nearly as exciting as it looks in cowboy films!

On the fourth Thursday in November, Americans celebrate U.S. Thanksgiving. Early settlers "gave thanks" for surviving in the New World.

△ **Native people** who lived along the north-west Pacific coast of Canada and the USA carved beautiful totem poles outside their homes.

When and where was the US railroad completed?
On May 10, 1869, a Union Pacific construction locomotive met one from the Central Pacific line, at a place called Promontory, in Utah. This completed a track that ran right across the United States.

▽ **Mexicans** celebrate many public holidays with a "fiesta." Then the streets are crowded with people.

NEW WORDS
Inuit Eskimo people of the Arctic regions.
New World North and South America, as it was seen as a new land by exploring Europeans.
Vikings Aggressive warriors from Norway, Sweden, and Denmark, who sailed in longships between the 8th and 11th centuries.

▷ **Football developed** from the British sport of rugby more than 100 years ago. The best college stars go on to play in the NFL.

FEATHER HEADDRESS
Cut a strip of corrugated paper and fit it around your head. Then stick the ends together with parcel tape. Tear colored tissue into small pieces, crumple the pieces up and glue them to the outside. Cut feather shapes from tissue and glue each one onto a plastic straw. Slot the ends into the corrugated holes to complete your headdress.

South America

The continent of South America is divided into 13 countries. By far the largest of these countries is Brazil, which covers nearly half the continent's total area.

The Andes Mountains stretch down almost the whole of South America. They form the longest mountain range in the world. The great Amazon River begins high in the Andes of Peru. It flows across the plains of Brazil, through the world's biggest rain forest, to the Atlantic Ocean.

▷ **The ruins** of the Inca town of Machu Picchu are perched high above a river valley in the Andes of Peru. A royal palace and a temple are among the ruins.

▷ **The Andes** mountain range is 7,200 km long. The highest point, called Aconcagua, is in Argentina.

◁ **A huge statue of Christ** looks down on the city and crowded beaches of Rio de Janeiro, in Brazil. The statue is 132 feet (40 m) high.

▽ **Llamas** are members of the camel family. They have been herded in Peru for thousands of years, for their wool and to carry things.

The Angel Falls, in Venezuela, is. the world's highest waterfall, falling to a depth of 3,212 feet (979 m).

▽ **In the thick Amazonian rain forest,** parrots and toucans feed in the treetops, while monkeys swing through the branches of this leafy canopy.

Brazil is the world's biggest producer of oranges, bananas, coffee, and sugarcane.

◁ **The southern tip of the continent** is called Cape Horn. It was named in 1616 by a Dutch explorer, after his home town of Hoorn in Holland. The Cape is usually very stormy.

The Atacama Desert stretches for almost 600 miles (1,000 km) along the Pacific coast of Chile. This is thought to be the driest place on Earth, because there is hardly ever any recorded rainfall at all.

NEW WORDS

plain A landscape with few trees.

range A group of mountains side by side.

215

South American People

The first Europeans arrived in South America in the 16th century. They then conquered and destroyed the powerful native American cultures they found there. The cultures included that of the mighty Inca empire.

Today, most South Americans are descended from Europeans and Indians, or native Americans, and many are a mixture of the two. Spanish is the continent's main language, but in the largest country, Brazil, people speak Portuguese. Native Americans also speak hundreds of Indian languages.

NEW WORDS

carnival A large festival with processions and fancy dress.

gaucho A cowboy and cattleman of Argentina.

native Americans The original people of North and South America, sometimes called Indians.

pampas Flat grassy lands of Argentina.

▽ **The Aymara people** traditionally live by farming and fishing from reed boats in Lake Titicaca. The lake lies high in the Andes, between Peru and Bolivia.

△ **Brazil** is famous for its friendly, crowded carnivals. They draw thousands of tourists every year. Many of the locals dress up in colorful costumes.

MAKE A SHAKER

Use an empty dishwashing liquid bottle or something similar. Put in some dried beans and push a stick into the neck of the bottle. Tape the stick so that it fits tightly. Paint the shaker with powder or poster paints mixed with a teaspoon of dishwashing liquid. Stick on some tissue-paper decorations with glue. Then shake to a South American beat.

Many people of the Amazon rain forest are losing their homeland as trees are cut down for timber and grazing land.

Big or Little Rain?

So much rain falls in the rain forest around the Amazon that Brazilians divide the seasons into times of "big rains" and "little rains." All this rain means that more than one fifth of all the water in the world's rivers flows down the River Amazon.

Soccer is the most popular sport in South America. Brazil has won the World Cup four times, and Uruguay and Argentina twice each.

▽ **Gauchos** are Argentinian cowboys, famous for their horsemanship. They herd cattle on grassy plains called pampas.

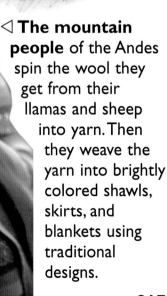

◁ **The mountain people** of the Andes spin the wool they get from their llamas and sheep into yarn. Then they weave the yarn into brightly colored shawls, skirts, and blankets using traditional designs.

217

Europe

The northern parts of Europe are mainly cold regions. They include Scandinavia, which is made up of Norway, Sweden, Finland, Denmark, and Iceland.

The central parts of the continent are mild, while the southern regions surrounding the Mediterranean Sea are mainly warm and dry. Europe has a rugged coastline, dotted with islands.

△ **In the Middle Ages,** important Europeans defended themselves in castles. Europe has many different types of castles.

Is the Black Sea black?
The waters of the Black Sea are not black, and it is a favorite vacation region. It may have got its name because heavy fog and sudden storms sometimes make it look dark. The ancient Romans called it the "Friendly Sea"!

▷ **There are many** active geysers, or hot springs, in Iceland. They regularly throw boiling hot water and steam high up into the air.

✗ **Icelanders** use hot water from beneath the Earth's surface to run power stations and heat their homes.

RE

◁ **The road across Tower Bridge,** in London, can open in the middle and swing up in the air. It does this so that tall ships can pass through and carry on up the River Thames. The rivers of Europe are important waterways.

PORTUGA
Lisbon ●

◁ **A popular tourist beach** on one of the many small islands off the mainland of Greece. In the summer it is warm and sunny all the way around the coast of the Mediterranean Sea.

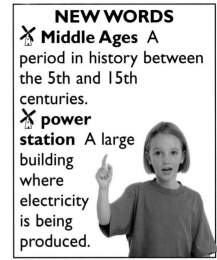

▷ **The Ural Mountains,** running across Russia, form an imaginary line separating the continents of Europe and Asia. Europe is well-known for its trade and industry.

NORWEGIAN SEA

C OCEAN

LAND

NORTH SEA

SWEDEN
FINLAND
NORWAY
Oslo
Helsinki
Stockholm
St. Petersburg
Archangel

R U S S I A

Nizhniy Novgorod

Moscow

ESTONIA
LATVIA
DENMARK
Copenhagen
LITHUANIA
BALTIC SEA

lin

UNITED KINGDOM
NETHERLANDS
London
BELGIUM
Paris
Seine
Loire
LUXEMBOURG
GERMANY
Berlin
Warsaw
POLAND
CZECH REPUBLIC
Danube
SLOVAKIA
Vienna
FRANCE
Lyon
AUSTRIA
Budapest
SWITZERLAND
HUNGARY
Milan
SLOVENIA
CROATIA
Po
BOSNIA-HERZEGOVINA
ANDORRA
Corsica
ITALY
YUGOSLAVIA
Barcelona
Rome
Sardinia
Naples
ALBANIA
MACEDONIA
Balearic Islands (Spain)
GREECE
Sicily
Athens

MINSK
Minsk
BELARUS
Kiev
UKRAINE
Dnieper
MOLDOVA
ROMANIA
Bucharest
BULGARIA
Sofia
Istanbul
Ankara
TURKEY

Don
Volga

KAZAKHSTAN

BLACK SEA

Rhône

ASIA

ORTH AFRICA

MEDITERRAN

219

∇ **Marching military bands** are a traditional feature of British ceremonies and special events. These soldiers are wearing fur helmets known as bearskins.

▷ **A gondolier,** or oarsman, rows his gondola along one of the many canals of Venice, in northern Italy. The water almost completely surrounds this beautiful city.

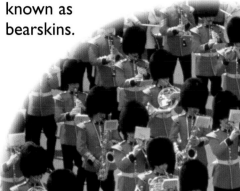

∇ **The grape harvest** is very important to many farmers and winemakers in France, Italy, Spain, and other southern European countries. In the past, people stamped on the grapes to press out the juice, but today the pressing is usually done by a special machine.

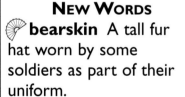

European People

Europe is full of many small countries and different peoples, most of whom have their own language and culture.

The north is home to Finns and Lapps, and to those who speak Germanic languages, such as the English, Dutch, and Germans. In the south, the French, Spanish and Italian languages all came from Latin, the language of the ancient Romans.

◁ **Flamenco** is a Spanish way of dancing and singing to guitar music. Dancers snap their fingers, clap their hands, and shout to the rhythmic music.

The world's smallest country is called Vatican City. It is the home of the Pope and lies in Rome, the capital of Italy.

△ **This square** is in Prague, the capital and largest city of the Czech Republic. The city's historic buildings attract many visitors all year round.

FAN YOURSELF

To make a Spanish fan, first paint or draw a bright pattern on a long sheet of paper. You could decorate it with glitter glue to add extra sparkle. When it is dry, fold the paper, makaing sure all the folds are the same size. Staple the folds at one end and then attach a popsicle stick as a handle for your fancy fan.

Asia

NEW WORDS

colony An area of land that people from another country control.

legend An old story handed down from generation to generation.

paddy field A flooded field where rice is grown.

Asia is by far the largest continent in the world, bigger than the whole of North and South America added together.

The Asian landscape varies from the huge, cold forest that stretches across northern Russia to the warm, wet rain forests of the islands of Southeast Asia. The world's highest mountains are also to be found in Asia.

△ **Rice** is an important food throughout Asia. It is grown in flooded paddy fields, like this one in Thailand. Sometimes fields are drained to help with harvesting.

▽ **The Himalayas,** a mountain range to the north of India, contain many of the highest mountains in the world. The highest of all, Mount Everest, rises to a height of about 29,028 feet (8,848 m).

◁ **Hong Kong** is an important port and city on the Chinese coast. This former British colony was returned to China in 1997.

▷ **The Great Wall of China** was built to help keep out invaders from the north. It was begun in about 200BC.

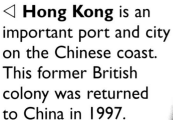 **Russia is the largest country** in the world. The Trans-Siberian Railroad runs all the way from the Russian capital, Moscow, to Beijing, the capital of China.

Where is the land of the rising sun?
The Japanese name for Japan, Nippon, means "source of the sun." A legend tells how an ancient god dipped his spear into the ocean and formed the islands of Japan from the sunlit droplets of water.

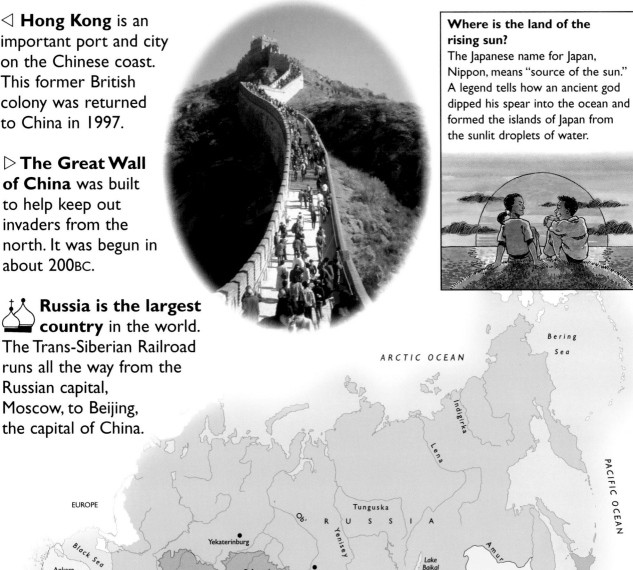

▷ **Japan** has more than 3,900 islands. Most of the islands of Southeast Asia are part of either the Philippines or of Indonesia.

223

Asian People

Over half the world's people live in Asia, which includes the country with more people than any other—China.

The world's first civilizations grew up in southwest Asia. In a fertile area between two great rivers, people grew crops and built big cities.

△ **The Mongols** of northern China and Mongolia are expert horse riders. They follow their herds of goats and cattle across the grasslands, living in felt tents called yurts.

NEW WORDS

fertile With rich soil, producing good crops.

nomads People who wander from place to place to find food and grazing land.

yurt A felt tent built and carried around by the Mongol people.

JAPANESE BEAUTY

You can easily make a simple Japanese flower arrangement in a bowl. Cover the bottom of the clear bowl with soil, then add gravel, shells, and pebbles. Push a small twig through the gravel into the soil. Half-fill the bowl with water. Then decorate the surface with leaves and flowers, to make simple Japanese beauty.

▷ **Very few people** live in the dry, hot Arabian Desert, but some Bedouin nomads wander around its edges. They herd camels and cattle, and live in dark tents.

Mount Everest lies between Nepal and Tibet. It was first climbed in 1953, by a Nepalese Sherpa called Tenzing Norgay and the New Zealander, Sir Edmund Hillary.

▽ **Fishermen** in Sri Lanka sit on pole perches in the shallow sea to fish.

△ **In China,** bike riding is a very popular way to get around the big cities quickly and easily. There are many large bicycle parks, with special attendants to look after them.

The Sultan of Brunei is said be the richest person in the world. He lives in a palace with 1,788 rooms. Brunei is a small country on the island of Borneo.

In Indonesia, on the island of Borneo, many families of the Dayak people live together in wooden longhouses.

▷ **Sumo** is the national wrestling sport of Japan. Sumo wrestlers are very big and strong, and they try to throw down their opponent or force him out of the ring to win.

Africa

Africa is the world's second largest continent. It is made up of 53 independent countries, some large and others small. The largest African country, Sudan, is more than 200 times bigger than the smallest, Gambia.

The Sahara is the biggest desert in the world. It covers more than a quarter of Africa and stretches for more than 3,000 miles (5,000 km)— from the Atlantic Ocean to the Red Sea. Farther south, the land is much more fertile with rain forests and grasslands.

▽ **There are many gold mines** in South Africa, which produces more of this precious metal than any other country in the world. It also mines diamonds.

▽ **Beautiful Egyptian boats** called feluccas sail on the River Nile, the longest river in the world. The Nile brings water and life to the desert countries that it flows through.

🐪 **In 1869** the Suez Canal was opened, joining the Red Sea to the Mediterranean Sea. This meant that ships could sail from Europe to the Indian Ocean without having to go right round Africa and the Cape of Good Hope. The canal is 105 miles (169 km) long and thousands of ships pass through it every year.

NEW WORD
🐪 **felucca** An Egyptian boat with one triangular sail.

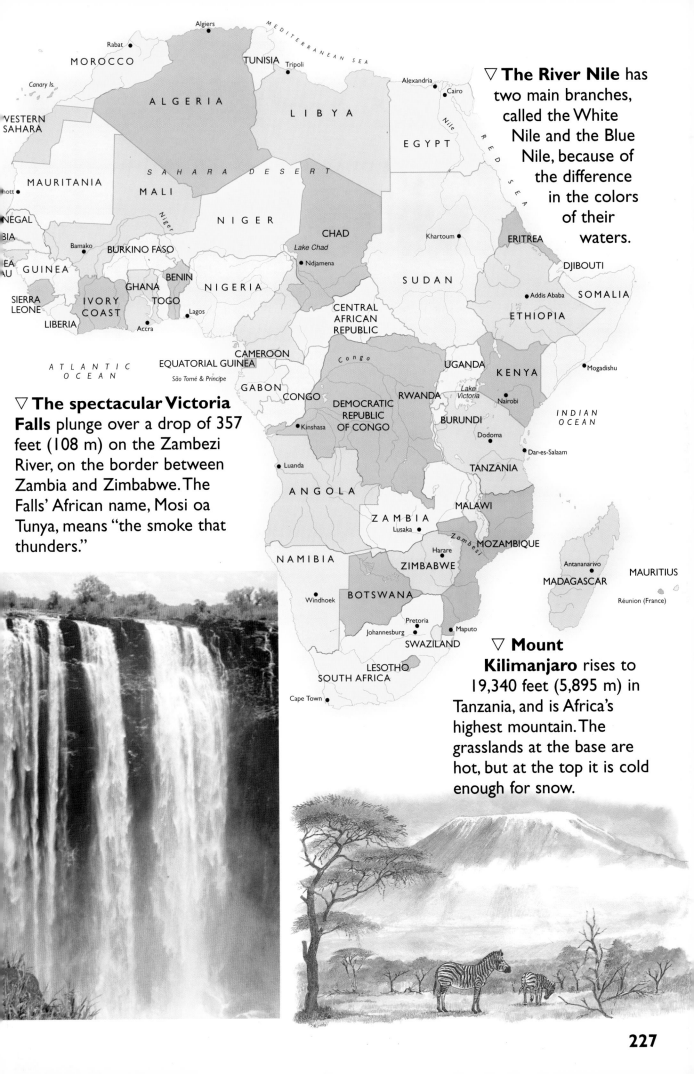

▽ **The River Nile** has two main branches, called the White Nile and the Blue Nile, because of the difference in the colors of their waters.

▽ **The spectacular Victoria Falls** plunge over a drop of 357 feet (108 m) on the Zambezi River, on the border between Zambia and Zimbabwe. The Falls' African name, Mosi oa Tunya, means "the smoke that thunders."

▽ **Mount Kilimanjaro** rises to 19,340 feet (5,895 m) in Tanzania, and is Africa's highest mountain. The grasslands at the base are hot, but at the top it is cold enough for snow.

MEDITERRANEAN SEA

MOROCCO
Rabat
Algiers
TUNISIA
Tripoli
ALGERIA
LIBYA
Canary Is.
WESTERN SAHARA
Alexandria
Cairo
EGYPT
SAHARA DESERT
MAURITANIA
MALI
NIGER
CHAD
Khartoum
ERITREA
Lake Chad
Ndjamena
DJIBOUTI
NEGAL
BIA
Bamako
BURKINO FASO
Niger
SUDAN
Addis Ababa
SOMALIA
EA AU
GUINEA
GHANA
BENIN
NIGERIA
CENTRAL AFRICAN REPUBLIC
ETHIOPIA
SIERRA LEONE
IVORY COAST
TOGO
Lagos
Mogadishu
LIBERIA
Accra
CAMEROON
EQUATORIAL GUINEA
Congo
UGANDA
KENYA
ATLANTIC OCEAN
São Tomé & Principe
GABON
CONGO
DEMOCRATIC REPUBLIC OF CONGO
RWANDA
Lake Victoria
Nairobi
INDIAN OCEAN
Kinshasa
BURUNDI
Dodoma
Dar-es-Salaam
Luanda
TANZANIA
ANGOLA
MALAWI
ZAMBIA
Zambesi
MOZAMBIQUE
Lusaka
Harare
Antananarivo
MAURITIUS
NAMIBIA
ZIMBABWE
MADAGASCAR
Réunion (France)
Windhoek
BOTSWANA
Pretoria
Johannesburg
Maputo
SWAZILAND
LESOTHO
SOUTH AFRICA
Cape Town

RED SEA

Nile

227

African People

▽ **These women** belong to a people called the Fulani, who live in West Africa. Many Fulani are still cattle herders, as they always have been, while others have moved to the cities for work.

Scientists believe that the earliest humans lived in Africa, millions of years ago. In more recent times, many African tribes and their lands were controlled by Europeans. Today, most African countries are completely independent.

Most Africans lived traditionally in villages and farmed the land. But the African population is growing very quickly, and many large cities have sprung up and continue to grow. Here there are modern offices and factories.

△ **Many Africans** still dress in a traditional way, according to the custom of their tribe.

NEW WORDS

independent
Governing itself and not controlled by other people.

pygmies
Members of various groups of small people.

tribe A group of people from the same race and with the same customs.

▷ **The streets** of many north African towns and cities are very crowded, and there are bustling markets. Marrakech, a large city in Morocco, is well known for its leather goods and textiles. These, and the warm climate, make it popular with tourists.

▽ **Johannesburg** is the largest city in South Africa and about four million people live there. It has many modern skyscrapers and shopping centers.

△ **Camels** are sometimes called the "ships of the desert," because they can go for a long time without water. Their humps are large stores of fat. Camels are a useful means of transportation, and can travel as far as 100 miles (160 km) in a day.

AFRICAN JEWELRY
Use felt pens to color macaroni and pasta wheels in stripes. Paint other pasta shapes with poster paints. When the shapes are dry, thread them onto about a metre of ribbon, varying the order of the shapes to make it look more interesting. Then try the necklace on—it should be easy to slip on and off. Finally, tie the ends of the ribbon with a double knot.

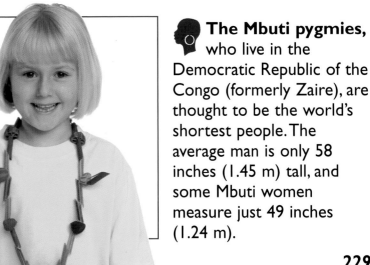

The Mbuti pygmies, who live in the Democratic Republic of the Congo (formerly Zaire), are thought to be the world's shortest people. The average man is only 58 inches (1.45 m) tall, and some Mbuti women measure just 49 inches (1.24 m).

229

Which lake has no water?
Lake Eyre, Australia's largest lake, is normally a huge area of mud covered with a crust of salt. This is because it is so hot and dry in the desert lands of South Australia. When there is very heavy rainfall, the lake does fill with water, but this is quite rare.

The Pacific Islands are in three main groups—Micronesia, which means "small islands," Melanesia ("black islands"), and, finally, Polynesia meaning "many islands."

▽ **Ayers Rock** rises 1,143 feet (348 m) above the surrounding dry plain. This giant rock is sacred to the Aborigines, who call it Uluru, which means "Earth mother."

Australasia

NEW WORDS

Aborigines The original people of Australia.

coral reef A large ridge in warm, shallow waters made up of a colony of tiny animals called corals.

outback The bush country of Australia, where desert land is partly covered by bushes and some trees.

The continent of Australasia is made up of Australia, New Zealand, Papua New Guinea, and thousands of small islands in the South Pacific Ocean. This region is sometimes called Oceania.

Australia is a warm, dry country and much of its land is desert and dry bush country, called outback. New Zealand has a milder climate. Both countries are home to many plants and animals seen nowhere else on Earth. The Pacific Islands cover a vast area, but most of them are very small.

△ **The roof** of the Sydney Opera House looks like giant sails. Sydney is the oldest and biggest city of Australia.

▷ **The Great Barrier Reef** lies off the coast of Australia. It is made up of thousands of coral reefs. The warm, shallow water is home to colourful fish.

Papua New Guinea covers the eastern half of New Guinea. The western half, called Irian Jaya, belongs to Indonesia.

Corals look like plants, but they are really made up of tiny, colorful animals. They are related to jellyfish.

231

Australasian People

The first Australians were Aborigines, who came from Asia about 40,000 years ago. They probably crossed land that is now under water, and wandered the desert, hunting and gathering food. The first European settlers arrived in 1788 and founded the city of Sydney.

Maoris were the first New Zealanders. According to a Maori legend, they sailed there from Polynesian islands in just seven canoes.

◁ **Aborigines** play a long, thick wooden pipe called a didgeridoo. This makes a deep note, and sometimes the player rests the pipe on a hole in the ground to make it sound louder. A boomerang, or throwing stick, is another traditional item.

PLAY A PIPE
Poke holes into one side of a cardboard tube. Then paint the tube. When it's dry, cover one end with wax paper, holding it in place with a rubber band. To play your pipe, hum into the open end as you move your fingers over the holes. A longer pipe makes a deeper note.

△ **Cricket** is a very popular sport in Australia and New Zealand. Many celebrated cricket players have come from those two countries.

Australia is the sixth biggest country in the world, but only 18 million people live there. Much of the land is hot, dry desert but most people live along the coasts.

▽ **Australian Aborigines** tell stories in their rock paintings. Many have been found that are thousands of years old.

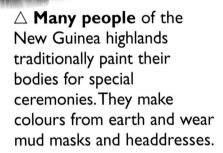

▽ **Wood carving** is a traditional craft of the Maoris of New Zealand. The carvings decorate Maori meeting houses. Today, much of the work is done to sell to tourists.

△ **Many people** of the New Guinea highlands traditionally paint their bodies for special ceremonies. They make colours from earth and wear mud masks and headdresses.

What day is it?
The international date line is an imaginary line that runs between the Pacific islands. On the western side of the line, it is exactly a day later than on the eastern side. So when it is midday Friday in Fiji, it is midday Thursday in Western Samoa.

NEW WORDS
🪃 **didgeridoo** A long, hollow, wooden pipe played by Aborigines.
🪃 **Maoris** The original people of New Zealand.
🪃 **pidgin English** A simple form of the English language.

◁ **Modern Australians** love the outdoor life. Surfing is popular off many beaches, along with swimming and sailing.

🪃 **The various peoples** of Papua New Guinea speak more than 700 different languages. Pidgin English and Motu are the most common languages.

MAKE A MUMMY

Take a doll and an old sheet. Tear the sheet into strips and wrap the doll from head to toe in these bandages. Make a coffin from a shoebox. The Egyptians put green stone scarab beetles along with their mummies, and you could paint one on the end of the coffin. When you want your doll back, just take the bandages off your Egyptian mummy!

⚠ When a body was mummified, the dead person's internal organs (liver, lungs, stomach and intestines) were removed and stored in special jars.

⚠ Cats were sacred to the ancient Egyptians and were also mummified when they died.

▷ **It probably took 100,000 men** more than 20 years to build the Great Pyramid. They used more than two million heavy blocks of stone. The pharaoh's burial chamber was deep inside the pyramid.

▽ **The wall paintings** found in ancient tombs have told us a lot about the way ancient Egyptians lived.

▷ **Pharaohs** were sometimes buried inside huge stone pyramids. The Great Pyramid is still standing at Giza, near Cairo, the modern capital of Egypt.

Ancient Egypt

Thousands of years ago, people hunted around the River Nile. Then they settled there and began to farm the land.

Ancient Egypt was ruled by kings, called pharaohs. The Egyptians believed the spirit of their hawk god, Horus, entered a new pharaoh and made him a god too. They also believed in life after death, and pharaohs were buried with things they wanted to take on to the next world.

△ **Egyptian noblemen** hunted in the marshes around the Nile. They used throwing sticks to bring down birds.

▷ **King Tutankhamun** died at only 18 years old. He was buried in a tomb in the Valley of the Kings, near the ancient city of Thebes. This gold mask was found among the treasure in Tutankhamun's tomb.

◁ **The stone monument** of the Great Sphinx has a man's head and a lion's body. It stands 66 feet (20 m) high, near the pyramids at Giza. The Sphinx was carved 4,500 years ago.

235

Ancient Greece

Hermes   Aphrodite   Zeus   Hera   Demeter   Hades

◁ **Zeus** was king of the Greek gods, and Hera was his wife. Hermes was the gods' messenger, Aphrodite was the goddess of love, Demeter goddess of grain, and Hades god of the dead.

About 2,800 years ago, a new civilisation began in Greece. The ancient Greeks produced many fine buildings and cities. They wrote plays, studied music, and began a system of government which allowed people a say in how their state was run.

Athens became the biggest and richest city state in ancient Greece, with a very well-trained army and a powerful navy. Sparta controlled the southern part of Greece. All true Spartans had to be warriors, and boys were trained to fight from the age of seven.

NEW WORDS

city state A state made up of a city and the surrounding areas.

column A pillar used to hold up a building.

government The ruling and running of a state or country.

state An organized community, such as a country.

trireme A warship with three banks of oars on each side.

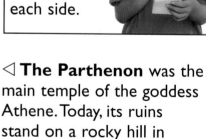

◁ **The Parthenon** was the main temple of the goddess Athene. Today, its ruins stand on a rocky hill in Athens called the Acropolis.

▷ **The Greeks** were the first to build permanent stone theaters. In ancient times the actors were all men, and they wore masks to show the sort of character they were playing.

Corinthian

Ionic

Doric

◁ **The ancient Greeks** developed special ways to decorate the tops of the columns, or pillars, that they used to support their beautiful buildings. Doric was the earliest order, or type. Then came Ionic, and finally Corinthian.

When and where were the first Olympic Games?
The first Olympic Games were held in 776 BC in Olympia, a place dedicated to the god Zeus. The first athletes carried shields and wore helmets, but no clothes!

DRAMATIC MASKS
Put a big plate on cardboard and draw around it. Then cut out the circle. Hold the cutout in front of your face and ask a friend to mark the position of your eyes. Put the cutout down and cut out two eye holes to see through. Paint a happy or a sad face, and tape on a popsicle handle. Finally, stick on card ears and ribbon hair.

Rich Greek boys had their own slave. It was his job to look after the boy, take him to school and help with his homework.

▷ **The most famous** types of Greek warship were biremes and triremes. A bireme had two banks of rowers on each side, and a trireme had three banks. Soldiers fought on the flat deck of the ships, which could go very fast and be used to ram others.

Ancient Rome

The great city of Rome began as a small village on one of seven hills, about 2,700 years ago. As the city grew in size and power, the Romans conquered other peoples in Italy.

Then the Roman armies created an empire that stretched around the Mediterranean Sea and reached as far as France and England. Roman soldiers built thousands of miles of good, straight roads throughout their empire. Some Roman roads still exist to this day.

▷ **The Roman Empire** began under Augustus, who became the first emperor in 27BC. This great leader set the style for later emperors.

🌿 **According to legend,** Rome was founded by two twins, Romulus and Remus. Abandoned as babies, the brothers were fed milk by a female wolf and later found by a shepherd.

🌿 **Roman cities** always had fresh water. It was brought from the hills to street fountains and houses along aqueducts.

△ **In AD79,** Mount Vesuvius suddenly erupted and covered the nearby Italian town of Pompeii with volcanic ash. The town was buried and thousands of people were killed.

What was the Roman circus?
In ancient Rome, the circus was an oval-shaped arena where chariot races were held. These were very popular sporting events, and up to 250,000 people could pack into the biggest circus in Rome.

▷ **Julius Caesar** was a great Roman general in the last years before the first emperor. He was stabbed to death in 44 BC.

▽ **The Forum** in ancient Rome was an open public square. Citizens went there to discuss any important questions of the day together.

▽ **The Colosseum** was the largest amphitheater of ancient Rome. It could hold about 50,000 spectators.

▷ **Centurions** were officers in the Roman army. Each one commanded about a hundred soldiers, who made up a century. The army was very well trained and extremely powerful.

The Middle Ages

The Middle Ages is the name that is usually given to roughly a thousand years of history, starting in about AD500. This medieval period covers the history between ancient and modern times in Europe.

During the Middle Ages, European countries were ruled by a king or an emperor, who generally owned all the land. The land was divided among the ruler's most important men, who were called nobles. The nobles were supported by knights, who were trained in battle. Peasants lived and worked on the nobles' and knights' land, growing food for both themselves and for their lord.

△ **Printing** had not yet been invented. Books were copied by hand by monks. They were often beautifully decorated in bright colors.

▽ **Kings and nobles** built castles to protect themselves against enemies. Inside they were often cold and damp, but there was always a large kitchen. Meals were eaten in the Great Hall.

△ **In medieval towns** there were no proper drains, and people threw their trash in the street. Jugglers, actors, and others put on entertainments, and there were shops selling all sorts of different goods.

▷ **Stained-glass windows** were used to decorate medieval churches. They often told stories from the Bible, using small pieces of colored glass held together by lead.

NEW WORDS

⬡ **knight** A man who was brought up to serve as a soldier.

⬡ **lance** A long spear.

⬡ **medieval** To do with the Middle Ages.

⬡ **noble** A person high up the social scale.

⬡ **peasant** A farmer or worker on the land.

⬡ **stained glass** Colored glass used in windows.

▽ **Knights** took part in tournaments, where they fought against each other on horseback. One knight tried to knock another to the ground by hitting him with his lance.

MAKE A CODE WHEEL

Cut out two cardboard circles, one smaller than the other. Mark them up with the 26 letters and numbers 0 to 9, and pin them together. To write a coded message, choose a key letter, say B. Turn the wheels until A on the outer wheel lines up with B on the inner. Write down the inner letters that line up with the outer letters in your message. To decode, a friend just has to set the wheel to the same key letter.

△ **Written Japanese** is based on ancient Chinese characters, but the Japanese symbols have developed differently. Japanese children also learn to write gracefully with a brush and ink. This beautiful writing is called calligraphy.

▷ **The ancient Egyptians** used a system of picture writing. Their symbols are called hieroglyphs.

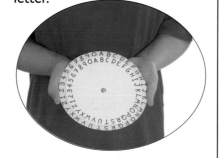

Can flags talk?
Flags can certainly be used to send messages. In the international flag code, there is a different flag for all 26 letters of the English alphabet. Sailors still sometimes use these to talk to others.

▷ **Arabic** is the main language of many Arab nations in the Middle East and northern Africa. The Arabic alphabet has 28 symbols and is written from right to left.

MANGER SQUARE

▽ **Russian** has its own alphabet. It has 33 letters and came originally from the Greek alphabet. Russian is related to the Polish and Czech languages.

▽ **Hindi** is the main official language of India, and there are 15 other important Indian languages too. Hindi words are linked with a line running across the top.

АБВГДЕЖЗИ
ЙКЛМНОПР
СТУФХЦЧШ
ЩЪЫЬЭЮЯ

△ **There are seven** different forms of spoken Chinese. The main form is called Mandarin, or Northern Chinese.

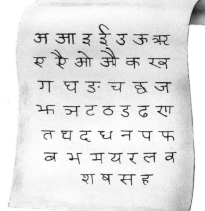

Languages of the World

SIGN LANGUAGE

Native Americans traditionally used sign language, because different tribes had their own spoken language. A sign language is made up of hand signals.

New Words

calligraphy A beautiful form of handwriting.

communicate To pass information to other people, often by talking.

hieroglyph A simple picture representing an object or a particular sound.

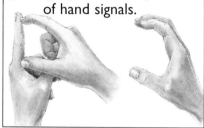

Language is made up of the words we speak or write down.
Words help us to communicate with each other, to tell each other things.

There are many different languages, and there are different alphabets for writing them down. People usually learn just one language when they are babies, but they can learn others when they are older.

△ **Here's how different people** say hello. From the left, the languages are English, Chinese, Spanish, Hindi, with Polish above.

▽ **This chart** shows the number of people who speak the world's major languages. Millions more people speak Chinese than English.

Chinese 845m
English 485m
Hindi 338m
Spanish 331m
Russian 291m
Arabic 192m
Bengali 181m
Portuguese 171m
German 138m
Japanese 124m
French 118m
Malay-Indonesian 117m

◁ **Written Chinese** does not have an alphabet of letters, but is made up of about 50,000 picture symbols. Each symbol, or character, stands for a word or part of a word. These Chinese children already know how to write thousands of characters.

Religions of the World

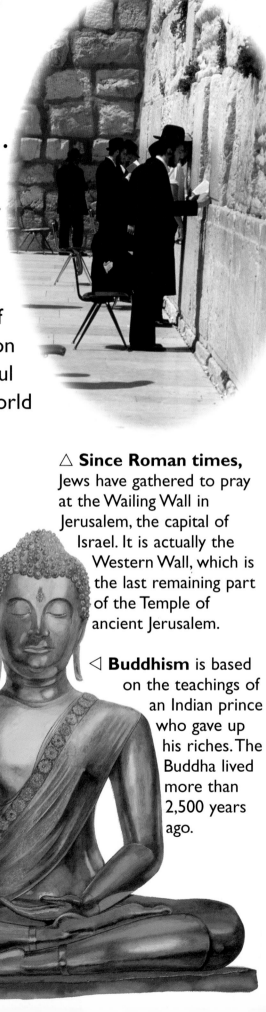

The world's main religions have existed for thousands of years. During this time, they have tried to explain the world and the meaning of life to their believers.

It is thought that over three quarters of the world's people follow a religion. Religion has been a powerful force in shaping world history, and has inspired many fine buildings, paintings, and music.

▽ **Many Christians** take their babies to church to be baptized, or christened. Babies usually have water sprinkled on them.

△ **Since Roman times,** Jews have gathered to pray at the Wailing Wall in Jerusalem, the capital of Israel. It is actually the Western Wall, which is the last remaining part of the Temple of ancient Jerusalem.

◁ **Buddhism** is based on the teachings of an Indian prince who gave up his riches. The Buddha lived more than 2,500 years ago.

NEW WORDS

baptize To receive a person into the Christian Church with a ceremony.

guru A religious teacher.

turban A head covering worn by Sikhs.

▷ **The River Ganges** is sacred to Hindus. They bathe in the river's waters to wash away their sins.

▽ **The Sikh religion** began in India more than 500 years ago. Sikh men wear a turban to keep their long, uncut hair in place. Sikhs follow the lessons of teachers called gurus.

▷ **Jerusalem** is a holy city for Jews, Muslims and Christians. For nearly three thousand years, the Jewish people have been closely linked to Jerusalem. The Dome of the Rock is the city's most holy Muslim Temple. The place where Muslims pray is called a mosque.

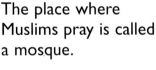

RELIGIOUS SYMBOLS

1. Siva, a Hindu god.

2. A Japanese Shinto temple.

3. A Jewish seven-branched candlestick, or menorah.

4. A Christian cross.

5. The crescent moon of Islam.

6. A Buddhist statue.

▽ **Buddhist monks** lead a simple, thoughtful life. They normally own nothing but their robes, a bowl, a razor, and a few personal belongings.

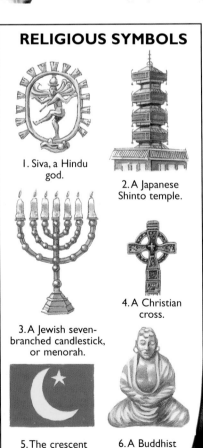

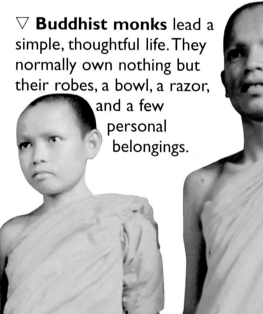

Festivals and Customs

Shrove Tuesday is also called Pancake Day in the UK. Making pancakes was a way of using up eggs and fat before the start of Lent, when people traditionally fast.

There are many different festivals all around the world. They usually celebrate a person or an event, and many of them happen once a year on special days called holidays.

Festivals are happy occasions, when people dance and dress up. Just like festivals, customs and traditions are handed down from one generation to the next. They are all things that are done the same way, year after year.

△ **Santa Claus** traditionally brings presents to children at Christmas. He is based on Saint Nicholas, who was a real bishop who lived more than 1,600 years ago.

▷ **In Mexico,** people remember their dead friends and relatives on the special Day of the Dead.

◁ **On the day of Halloween,** October 31, children dress up in ghostly costumes, make jack-o-lanterns, and play trick-or-treat. It is a day for stories about ghosts, witches, and wizards.

▽ **Dragon dancers** weave their way through the streets, celebrating Chinese New Year. This is a time for family parties.

HALLOWEEN FRIEZE
Copy the shapes of a witch, a moon, a bat, an owl, and other dark or ghostly things on colored paper and cut them out. Draw in eyes, stick on decorations, and glue the shapes onto a large piece of paper or cardboard. Sprinkle with glitter for a star-spangled Halloween finish, and put it up in your room.

△ **The world's most famous carnival** is held for four days every year in Rio de Janeiro, Brazil. There are street parades, costume parties, and dances.

🎇 **In China**, the end of the New Year season is celebrated by having a special Lantern Festival.

Quiz

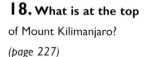

1. What is the name of the largest gorge in the world? *(page 210)*

2. Which is the largest state in the USA? *(page 211)*

3. What does the name of the Inuit people mean? *(page 212)*

4. In which year was the railroad across America completed? *(page 213)*

5. Which is the largest country in South America? *(page 214)*

6. What is the world's highest waterfall called? *(page 215)*

7. What is the main language of South America? *(page 216)*

8. Who are gauchos? *(page 217)*

9. Which countries make up Scandinavia? *(page 218)*

10. Which mountains separate Europe and Asia? *(page 219)*

11. In which city can you see gondoliers? *(page 220)*

12. What is the name of a traditional Spanish dance? *(page 221)*

13. Which is the world's biggest continent? *(page 222)*

14. Why was the Great Wall of China built? *(page 223)*

15. Which country has more people than any other? *(page 224)*

16. What is the traditional form of Japanese wrestling called? *(page 225)*

17. Which two seas are joined by the Suez Canal? *(page 226)*

18. What is at the top of Mount Kilimanjaro? *(page 227)*

19. Where do scientists believe the earliest humans lived? *(page 228)*

20. What are "ships of the desert"? *(page 229)*

21. What are the three groups of Pacific Islands called? *(page 230)*

22. Where is the Great Barrier Reef? *(page 231)*

23. Who were the first Australians? *(page 232)*

24. What is the international date line? *(page 233)*

25. What was inside the Great Pyramid? *(page 234)*

26. Which famous ancient Egyptian king died at the age of 18? *(page 235)*

27. Who was king of the ancient Greek gods? *(page 236)*

28. What did the first Olympic athletes wear? *(page 237)*

29. Who was the first Roman emperor? *(page 238)*

30. How many soldiers did a Roman centurion command? *(page 239)*

31. When were the Middle Ages? *(page 240)*

32. What weapons did knights carry in tournaments? *(page 241)*

33. How many letters are there in the Russian alphabet? *(page 242)*

34. What is the Spanish for "hello"? *(page 243)*

35. Where did the Buddha come from? *(page 244)*

36. Which river is sacred to Hindus? *(page 245)*

37. What is another name for Pancake Day? *(page 246)*

38. Where is the world's most famous carnival held? *(page 247)*

Index

253

· ·

ACKNOWLEDGMENTS

The publishers wish to thank the following artists who have contributed to this book:

Julie Banyard Page 81 (R), 82 (TL), 85 (TR);
Martin Camm 138-39 (B), 139 (TR), 143 (CR), 145 (CL), 146 (BR), 149 (CL), 151 (TC, CR), 158 (T), 159 (C), 167 (TL, CL);
Mike Foster (The Maltings Partnership) 14 (BL, T), 23 (BR), 29 (TL), 35 (BR), 37 (CR), 47 (C), 54 (BR), 57 (CR), 59 (B), 69 (BR), 72 (TL), 76 (CL), 79 (TR), 95 (BL), 101 (TR), 102 (BR), 104 (CB), 104-105 (T), 113 (CR), 114 (BR), 124 (BR), 135 (CR), 137, 141 (CR), 143 (TR), 151 (C), 155 (CL), 161 (BL), 166 (TL), 213 (CT), 217 (TR), 218 (CL), 223 (TR), 230 (TL), 233 (CR), 237(TR), 238 (BR), 242 (CL), 243 (T, CR), 246 (CL), 171 (CL), 176 (BL), 179 (CB, BL), 180 (CR), 182 (TL), 185 (BL, BR), 119 (CL), 195 (TL), 198 (CL), 200 (CL), caption icons throughout;
Ron Hayward 55 (L), 63 (C), 80 (B), 81 (B); 214 (BL), 218 (CR), 227 (BR), 242 (BL, CB, BR), 243 (CL), 244 (B), 245 (CR), 246 (BR);
Gary Hincks 30 (T), 31 (BR), 32 (B), 37 (T), 39 (C);
Richard Hook 237 (B, CR);
Rob Jakeway 12; 234 (TR);
Steve Kirk 171 (TL), 177 (B), 181 (BR), 196 (TR, C), 197 (T, C, B), 200-201 (B);
Janos Marffy 211 (C), 215 (CT), 219 (B), 223 (B), 227 (T), 230 (B);
Mel Pickering (Contour Publishing) 10 (BL), 11 (CL), 13 (T), 14 (C), 15 (BR), 18 (C), 21 (TR), 25 (BR), 27 (C), 32 (TL), 33 (TR), 52 (B), 53 (C, CB), 68 (C), 178 (TL), 181 (CT), 186 (T), 187(C), 206(B);
Gillian Platt (Illustration Ltd.) 114 (CR), (CL), 131 (BL), 141 (B), 153 (C), 155 (R), 164 (C), 165 (C);
Terry Riley 35 (T), 42 (T), 69 (TL), 131 (TR), 133 (C), 134 (C), 135 (T), 136 (C), 136-137 (C), 140 (B), 147 (CR), 148 (CL), 152 (C), 154 (B), 155 (BL), 170 (BL), 172-173 (B), 174-175(B), 179 (CB, BL), 180 (BL), 182 (TR), 189 (T), 194-195 (B), 198 (B), 203 (T, CT,TR);
Mike Saunders 91 (BR), 92 (R), 95 (TR), 97 (TR), 99 (TR), 101 (B), 104 (L), 107 (TR, B), 108 (BL), 110 (R), 115 (BL), 116 (CL), 118 (C), 119 (C), 123 (C);
Guy Smith (Mainline Design) 16-17(C, B), 40 (C), 57 (BR), 58 (T, B), 59 (R), 60 (BR), 66 (BR), 68 (TR), 71 (TL, BR), 74-75 (all), 76 (C), 78 (L), 79 (TL), 91 (C), 92 (CL), 93 (L), 94 (CR), 95 (CL), 96 (L), 99 (BL), 100 (BR), 103 (CR), 109 (CR), 114 (CB), 116 (TR), 118 (BL), 119 (CR), 120 (CR, BR), 122 (TL, BR), 126 (BL, CB);
Roger Stewart 53 (T), 62 (L), 63 (BL, BR), 67 (TR, CR), 69 (TC), 72 (C), 73 (BR), 117 (TL), 159 (TR);
Michael Welply 240 (B), 241 (T);
Michael White (Temple Rogers) 13 (BR), 21 (L), 44 (BL), 64-65 (B), 160 (BR), 172 (CR), 173 (T), 177 (CR), 182-183 (CB), 185 (CL, CR), 187 (BR), 188 (BR), 191 (B), 195 (TR), 196 (B), 202-203 (B), 212 (BL), 213 (BR), 216 (BR), 217 (CR), 220-221 (CB), 224 (TL), 225 (CR), 232 (CL, CR), 236 (T), 238 (TR), 239 (CR), 241 (BR), 245 (BL), 246 (TR);
Michael Woods 141 (CL), 142 (B), 148 (CR), 150 (BL), 151 (CL), 158 (B), 160 (TL), 162 (CR), 163 (C).

The publishers wish to thank the following for supplying photographs for this book:

AKG Page 239 (CL);
Chris Bonington Library 24 (B)/Doug Scott;
Susanne Bull 87 (T);
Corbis 171 (B), 199 (B), 200 (TR), 206 (TR), 207 (TR);
E.T. Archive 241 (CR);
Honda Dream solar car 70 (T);
Gerard Kelly 85 (B);
Miles Kelly archives 18 (BR), 19 (B), 20 (T), 29 (B), 31 (TL, TR), 32 (C), 34 (B), 36 (T, B),
38 (TL, BL, B, BR), 40 (BL), 41 (TR), 42 (B), 43 (TR, CR), 44 (C), 45 (T), 46 (TR), 52 (TR), 53 (L, TR),
54 (TR, BL), 55 (TR, BR), 56 (TR, C, B), 57 (T), 60 (BL), 61 (T), 25 (TR, CR), 66 (C), 67 (BL), 68 (L),
69 (TR, TC below), 70 (B), 72 (TR, BR), 73 (TR, CR, CL), 79 (BR), 80 (T, CL, CR), 81 (CL), 82 (TR, B),
83 (T, CL, CR, BR), 84 (C, BL, BR), 85 (TL), 86 (TR, TL, C, B), 87 (CL, CR, B), 93 (TR, BL), 95 (BR),
97 (CL), 98 (TL, C), 100 (BL), 103 (C, BL), 106 (TL, TR, CT, CL), 108 (TR), 111 (TR, CR, BL), 112 (TR),
113 (TL, C, CL), 114 (TR), 117 (TR), 118 (BR), 119 (CT), 122 (CL), 123 (TR, BR), 124 (TR, CR),
125 (TL, TR, CR, BL), 127 (TR, BR); 130 (BL, TR, CR), 131 (TL, MR), 132 (TL, B), 133 (T, CL, CR),
134 (TL, BL, TR), 135 (BL), 136 (TL, TR), 137 (TL, CL, TR), 138 (CL, TR), 139 (CL, CR), 140 (TR),
141 (TR), 142 (TL, BR), 143 (TL), 144 (TL, BL), 145 (TR, B), 146 (TR, BL), 147 (TL, BL), 148 (TR, B),
149 (T, TL, TR, C, BL, BR), 150 (TL), 151 (TL, B), 152 (TL, TR, CB), 153 (TR), 154 (TL, CR), 155 (TL),
156 (CL, BR, TR), 157 (TL, BR, C, TR), 159 (TR, BR), 161 (BL, TL, C, CL), 162 (CL, BR, TR),
163 (CL, C, TR, CR), 164 (TR, TL, CR, BL), 165 (BL, CR, TR), 166 (TR, BL, CR), 167 (TR, CR),
170 (TL), 171 (TR), 173 (CL, CR), 175 (TR), 178-79 (CB), 180 (CT), 183 (T), 184 (CR, B), 185 (CB),
186 (TR, C, CL, CB, CR), 187 (TL, CL), 189 (BL, BR), 192 (TL, BL), 192-93 (B), 193 (C), 199 (T), 201 (CR),
202 (TR), 204 (BR), 210 (CL, BL), 211 (CR), 212 (TL), 213 (CL, CR), 214 (BR, CR), 214-15 (CT), 216 (CL),
217 (TR), 218 (BL), 219 (TL, BL), 220 (TL), 221 (CL, TR), 221-22 (C), 222 (TR), 223 (TR, CL, B), 224 (CT),
226 (TR, CL, BR), 227 (CR, BL), 228 (BL), 229 (BL, TR), 230 (CL), 231 (TR), 232 (C, BR),
234 (TR, TL, CL), 235 (BL, CR, BR), 236 (TR, BR), 237 (BL), 239 (CB), 240 (TR, B), 241 (TL),
243 (TR, C, CR), 245 (TR), 246 (TR, BR), 247 (BL), 248 (T, CR);
Natural Science Photos 178 (BL), 179 (TR), 186 (BL), 188 (TR), 191 (T), 201 (CL), 207 (CL, CR, BL,);
Panos 229 (TR, CR);
PhotoDisc 10 (TL), 11 (R), 21 (B), 22 (L, B), 23 (TR), 26 (CT);
Rex Features 28 (T, BL), 45 (BR)/Greenpeace/Tim Baker, 46 (TR), 47 (TL, TR);
78 (CR)/The Times/Simon Walker;
Sega Rally 77 (TR);
Science Photo Library 77 (BR)/Geoff Tomkinson 115 (C);
Patrick Spillane (Creative Vision) 100 (CR), 109 (BL), 115 (T);
The Stock Market 20 (B), 21 (TR), 35 (C), 42 (BL), 47 (BR), 50 (TL, B), 51 (BR), 54 (C), 63 (T)
105 (TL), 111 (BL), 117 (B), 120 (TR), 126 (CR), 233 (CB), 243 (BL), 244 (CL), 245 (CL);
Tony Stone Images 93 (CR).

All model photograhy by **Mike Perry at David Lipson Photography Ltd.**

Models in this series:
Lisa Anness, Sophie Clark, Alison Cobb, Edward Delaney, Elizabeth Fallas,
Ryan French, Luke Gilder, Lauren May Headley, Christie Hooper,
Caroline Kelly, Alice McGhee, Daniel Melling, Ryan Oyeyemi, Aaron Phipps,
Eriko Sato, Jack Wallace.
Clothes for model photography supplied by:
Adams Children's Wear